SHEPHERDING THE FLOCK

Shepherding the Flock

Problems of pastoral discipline in the Early Church
and in the younger churches today

*The James Long Lectures 1965
delivered on behalf of the Church
Missionary Society*

by

S. L. GREENSLADE

*Regius Professor of
Ecclesiastical History,
University of Oxford*

SCM PRESS LTD
BLOOMSBURY STREET LONDON

First published 1967
© SCM Press Ltd 1967
Printed in Great Britain by
Billing & Sons Limited
Guildford and London

CONTENTS

PREFACE

JAMES LONG WAS a much respected missionary in Calcutta who died in 1887, leaving money to endow lectures of which Eugene Stock could write in 1916 that they had been delivered ever since by missionaries who were real experts. So far from being an expert one, I am no missionary at all; I am all the more grateful to the Church Missionary Society for the invitation to give the lectures in 1965. Shortly before he ceased to be General Secretary, Dr M. A. C. Warren suggested that, in view of the constant disciplinary problems which beset the younger churches, I should review the disciplinary system of the early Church, with some exploration of its relevance today. These lectures therefore issue from my professional work on the early Church, though experts will soon detect how often I have been compelled to glide over historical problems. I am acutely aware how slight is my acquaintance (even by book-knowledge) with the life of the churches overseas. I have tried to remedy this superficiality a little by concentrating my reading somewhat upon Africa where all the problems seem to be represented.

I do not suggest that the early Church provides a pattern of discipline directly applicable to any modern situation; but it was then the younger Church, compared with Israel, and a missionary Church in a pagan environment. Its experiences, problems and struggles deserve study by those who are responsible for similar decisions today. I would add that, conversely, my own study of the early Church has been much refreshed by looking at it in the light of what I have now been reading about the younger churches of the present.

I am deeply grateful to Dr Warren and his successor, Dr J. V. Taylor, for their encouragement.

S. L. G.

I did as a matter of fact do what was the practice of the early Christians. . . . It is so easy to see how the discipline of the early Church was not an artificial, but a necessary system, though by degrees elaborated in a more complicated manner. But I find, not seldom, that common sense dictates some course which afterwards I come across in Bingham, or some such writer, described as a usage of the early Christians. In our English nineteenth century life such practices could hardly be reintroduced with benefit. Yet something which might mark open offences with the censure of the Christian Body is clearly desirable when you can have it; and of course with us there is no difficulty whatever.

John Coleridge Patteson, *Bishop in Melanesia*, 1869

CHAPTER ONE

THE HOLINESS OF THE CHURCH IN A PAGAN SOCIETY

'Come out from among them, and be ye separate.'

I

I POSSESS a standard *History of South-East Asia*, 800 pages long. Its extensive index refers to the Netherlands Steam Navigation Company, but not to the Netherlands Missionary Society. The book says much of Java, but you will not find the names of Coolen or Medhurst or Jellesma. Conrad Coolen, son of a Dutch father and a Javanese mother of noble family, was a planter, patriarchal and high-handed, who built up a Christian community on his estate at Ngoro. He had his own methods: he had expert knowledge of the traditional puppet-plays of Java, and adapted them to portray bible stories; he composed prayers and hymns to be recited in the traditional Javanese manner, and devised Christian ceremonies in a Javanese style to mark and sanctify the harvest and the events of the farmer's year. But he thought the biblical and historic sacraments, baptism and eucharist, unnecessary. Indeed he was afraid of baptism, fearing that with it his converts would break away from their own culture and try to be Dutch.

Medhurst was an English Missionary who in 1841 visited Wijung, an offshoot from Ngoro. His outlook was altogether different. He asked them pointblank whether they had broken completely with Islam, found that they meant to circumcise their children at the age of thirteen so that they might marry their neighbours, and that they were prepared still to acknowledge

Mohammed as an Apostle of God with their lips, though not in their hearts. Medhurst taught them that they could not compromise and must risk the consequences of a clean break with their neighbours and their ways. Then he visited Coolen at Ngoro, where he listened in dismay to the low sing-song drawling of the creed which took twenty minutes and had a suspicious response, 'There is one God, and Jesus Christ is the spirit of God.' He condemned the Javanese plays and told Coolen to keep closer to Scripture.

Here are conflicting views of the process of Christianization. For one, Christian life will be nourished by getting inside and using the traditional culture; for the other, the Bible and the Church demand and provide a new way of life which can flourish and propagate itself only when a clean sweep of the old is made. 'Come out from among them, and be ye separate.' When Jellesma, a Dutch pastor, arrived, he took a middle line. Christians in Java should be truly Javanese, not imitation Dutchmen, but they must be built up into a genuine church, taking account of those biblical demands which require a Christian to be different from his neighbour and ready to make sacrifices. Perhaps this sounds sensible and simple; but to put it into practice he had to start afresh and found a third community—from which he had before long to excommunicate a leader who was organizing parties of dancing-girls![1]

Throughout the centuries Christian history has faced the problem: assimilation or separation, or some compromise. In the early Church it is the note of separation which stands out most clearly, though the full truth is complex. The Old Testament gave them two pictures. In one they saw the People of God more or less comfortably settled in the Promised Land, able to develop their own institutions and ways of life on the accepted basis of the word and law of the Lord God whom alone they worshipped and served. The whole community, not the church in particular, could

---

[1] K. S. Latourette, *History of the Expansion of Christianity*, V, pp. 291-93; E. A. Payne, *South-East from Serampore*; and information from the Rev. D. Bentley-Taylor.

be envisaged as holy unto the Lord. At their best, secular and religious authorities — though the distinction is misleading — worked together to protect the people from contamination by other cultures and foster a godly life. If the king betrayed his duty, prophet or priest would recall him to it; if they went astray, the king could call them to account. The other picture showed the People of God oppressed by conquering nations, tempted to conform to their religions and cultures. In Babylon the Jews must be exhorted to loyalty; they must witness to their faith at whatever cost in suffering, they must hold tenaciously to their national and religious laws and traditions. To be holy now means to separate themselves from the surrounding culture. 'Depart ye, depart ye, go ye out from thence, touch no unclean thing; go ye out of the midst of her; be ye clean, ye that bear the vessels of the Lord' (*Isa. 52.11*). God will soon release them from exile, but they must come out clean.

Three or four centuries later, after a period when the Jews in Palestine were tempted to interpret their holiness to the Lord too narrowly, they were put to another test by the attractions of Greek culture and the ambition of Antiochus Epiphanes, King of Syria, to erect a great kingdom cemented by a uniform way of life, Greek of course. Though Greek thoughts, Greek buildings, dress, athletics and other customs set their spell upon some, especially young men fretting at an illiberal traditionalism, the threat to the Temple and the Law sparked off the Maccabaean Revolt, and by its success the people could again be preserved in the way of holiness, whatever cultural separation that must imply. There were fresh troubles when the Romans came, and there were always some who wanted compromise, but on the whole their distinctive morality and manners, grounded in a distinctive religion and controlled by the Mosaic Law as expounded by the rabbis, was faithfully maintained under the leadership of the Pharisees. And on the fringe were the extremist groups ranging from Zealots who preached political action against Rome to Essenes who thought complete purity could only be attained in physical isolation from the populous centres of ordinary Jewish life. Many expected that God would soon break-in to establish his kingdom.

II

The earliest Christians had to ponder the lessons of Jewish history and elicit from the Jewish Scriptures, which they adopted, guidance for the Christian Way in its actual circumstances. First, how different should they be from the Jews themselves? Must Christians be circumcised? How far is the Law binding on them? The New Testament reveals anxious struggles with this grave problem. Since circumcision was a kind of sacrament of the old covenant and carried with it the obligation to observe the Law, the decision that Christians need not be circumcised was crucial: a Christian need not first become a Jew. St Paul made it plain that salvation comes not by works of the Law but by faith in Christ, that there is a Christian freedom from law. St John spoke of the new commandment of love which Jesus laid upon us. Yet God had truly made Israel his people and revealed himself to them and given them his Law, which all Christians must take seriously. Christian morality would certainly start from Jewish morality and the teaching of the Old Testament, even if it brought a new spirit into it. Though there would be problems about the Law, agreement of Jew and Christian on many fundamental moral issues would separate both of them from the manners and morals of the Graeco-Roman world.

So the problem came up in its second form. How different must the Gentile Christian be from his Greek or Roman or other neighbour across the street? On some points of morality the difference would be evident enough. To take a simple example, the Christian seriously believed that fornication is wrong, and for a man as well as a woman. But subtler problems would arise, some of which do not seem to have worried the middle-of-the-road Jew. Could a Christian be rich, if it is so hard for a rich man to be saved? Can a Christian go to war? How strait is the gate that leads to life? Must they be few who find it? The problems were not all moral. The Jew thought like a Jew; his religion and language and mental outlook had become a homogeneous whole.[2] The Christian convert came as a Hellenistic Greek from Egypt or Syria or Asia Minor, from Thessalonica or Athens or Corinth, as a Latin from Rome, in time as a Latinized Berber, a Celtic-speaking Gaul, a Briton, a German. He came into a new world of thought. In what sense must he come out of his former structure of thought and feeling? Would Latin or Greek philosophy help to elucidate the Christian Gospel and its implications for society, or were they bound to corrupt its essence? And could the less sophisticated pagan make the effort of imagination required to grasp a message born of and expressed in the terms of another culture? Would he not be transforming it, in his heart of hearts, to something nearer his own tradition? Above all, the convert must be separated from idolatry. No one questioned the principle; but how apply it in an environment where manners as well as morals, the whole fabric of society, had an idolatrous pattern and texture?

St Paul often grappled with such matters. In Colossians he must stave off harmful ideas about Christ which probably came from an amalgamation of Jewish and pagan notions of the universe, and in I Corinthians he defends the foolishness of preaching Christ crucified against the wisdom or philosophy of the world and the Greeks who seek it. He has also to take up concrete problems about idolatry: eating meat which has been sacrificed to an idol, sitting at meat in an idol temple Consistency was not easy. There is a Christian liberty of conscience, but it must not be so exercised as to scandalize the conscience of a weaker brother. The idol is nothing, but 'I would not that ye should have communion with demons'. 'All things are Christ's,' but they are not all acknowledged to be his; there are dangers in keeping company with pagans who claim them for other gods. How far Paul could go in his fear of contamination comes out in II Corinthians 6.14-7.1, now commonly believed to be a fragment of another letter:

Be not unequally yoked with unbelievers; for what fellowship have righteousness and iniquity? or what communion hath light

[2] Essentially true, but a simplification. There were differences among Jews, especially in degree of Hellenization.

with darkness? And what concord hath Christ with Belial? . . .
Wherefore [and he uses the Isaiah passage] Come ye out from
among them, and be ye separate, saith the Lord, and touch not the
unclean thing.

This might be thought to prescribe physical as well as moral
separation from the pagan world, and so it was understood by
some, if I Cor. 5.9 is correcting this interpretation: I wrote to you
not to associate with immoral men. I did not mean the immoral of
this world, or idolators, since then you would have to go out of
the world. I meant brothers who fall into immorality or idolatry
— not even to eat with them. In other words, Paul had been talking
about discipline *within* the Church, which we must consider later.
The problem of social intercourse with pagans remained open.

The early Church did not make a deliberate choice between
alternative theories of how to deal with the world, namely Chris-
tianizing it or getting out of it, for in practice they had little
option. The Old Testament picture of a homogeneous community
agreed in worship, accepting God's Law as the basis of the common life under the leadership of the king — could a handful of
Christians dream of translating that into a Christian Roman
Empire? Possibly, if their perspective allowed enough time; but
it did not, for most of them believed that Christ would soon
return in judgment, that this age would pass away in a few years.
It might last a few decades, certainly not centuries. The Gospel
must be preached, but the object was to rescue men and women
from this world to eternal salvation through Christ. There would
not be time for Christian converts, however new their way of life,
to revolutionize society in general.

This outlook is individualistic, in a way, and world-renouncing.
Still, the individuals saved from the world were gathered into a
close fellowship, one Spirit and one body, universal but made
visible and concrete in local communities: they must meet together for worship and instruction and mutual support, and their
conduct must make them visibly distinct from their neighbours.
They are called to holiness, essentially a holiness to God, the self-
offering in Christ of those who belong to God, a Godward move-

ment. At the same time there is a manward movement of witness:
'Let your light so shine before men that they may see your good
works and glorify your Father which is in heaven.' So Christian
individual and community must be kept holy, with all the separation required from time to time and place to place, even to the
point of martyrdom. Unlike the Victorian missionary in Africa,
they were not coming as agents of civilization with gifts of
literacy, education, medicine, technology, commerce, and they
were not backed by political authority. They had only their truth
to offer, the Gospel, the Word of God, together with a way of life
flowing from the Gospel, seen at first in the individual, the family
and the closed Christian group; only gradually could this become
a civilizing force, and they had no time for the inevitability of
gradualness.

III

Since I cannot describe in detail how the Church worked out its
notion of separateness, it will be best to jump on to one example,
extreme, yet by its vigour pointing up the problems inescapably:
the writings of Tertullian, a presbyter at Carthage about AD 200.
In one work (*De Spectaculis*) he forbade Christians to attend the
theatre or other public shows, partly because they were often
immoral, even more because they were riddled with idolatry,
whether by the content of a play or the idolatrous ceremonies
which accompanied the shows. They belonged to the devil, his
pomp and his angels, precisely what a Christian had renounced at
baptism. It's no use agreeing (he says) that you won't go to anything that's expressly forbidden in the Bible while holding yourself
free to see anything else. Get to the root of the matter. Is it the kind
of thing that belongs to the devil? It's no good saying you don't
believe in the pagan gods and won't be taking part in idolatry, but
only looking on. You'll be dragged down somehow; all shows do
violence to the spirit. Anyhow, you will be failing in Christian
witness, for other people won't understand your subtleties. They
know that a man has become a Christian when he gives up the
games; that's his mark. So Tertullian quotes St Paul: 'What com-

munion hath light with darkness, life with death?' and coins a
neat epigram: *saeculum dei est, saecularia autem diaboli* – the
world belongs to God, but worldly things to the devil. A book on
military service (*De Corona Militis*) has a similar argument. A
Christian cannot be a soldier because he will come under orders
which are both immoral (shall the son of peace fight in battle?)
and idolatrous (shall he guard the temples he has renounced?). He
cannot take the oath (*sacramentum*) of obedience to Caesar and
the baptismal vow (*sacramentum* again) which renounces the devil
and makes him Christ's alone. Shall he ask a watchword from
the emperor when he already has one from God?

Tertullian gathered his thoughts into a comprehensive treatise
On Idolatry, which we might have called *The Church and the
World.*[3] Granted that Christians do not worship idols, what does
this involve practically in a heathen environment? First, you cannot make them, as painter or sculptor. It's no good saying, this is
the craft I was brought up to, I've nothing else to live by. Examine
yourself, and you'll admit you are not being honest. You can
adapt your skill to something similar; there are plenty of markets.
And don't argue that St Paul said, 'Let everyone continue as he
was found.' We cannot stay in our sins. Craftsmen must also take
care that their products, harmless in themselves, are not being
bought for use in temples. If we fail to take normal precautions,
we are not clear of the infection of idolatry. From this he turns
to condemn all magic, divination and astrology – a warning still
relevant – and then swings abruptly round to schoolmasters. They
must praise the gods and tell children about them and share their
fees with Minerva. Can a Christian teach on such terms? Tertullian thought not, though others of his time took a different
line (they might manage to undermine belief in them, they might
vituperate the gods). But in view of the impracticability of Christian schools when persecution always threatened, he allows Christian children to attend pagan schools, provided they are first

[3] For a translation with some further discussion see my *Early Latin
Theology* (Library of Christian Classics V, SCM Press, 1956), pp. 78-
110.

taught what idolatry is, since they must get some education. The unusual concession implies perhaps that most Christian parents could not have given them much education at home.

Returning for a moment to craftsmen and shopkeepers in order to condemn Christian incense-merchants whose wares, though useful for medicine or burials, were more likely to find their way into temples, he next considers various festivals and social celebrations. Naturally the Christian will not participate as priest or sacrificer or worshipper in specifically religious festivals, but there are some which might trap the unwary. He might give presents on days which only became gift-days because they are dedicated to a pagan god, or take a holiday for the same reason. He must not; that is a taint of idolatry, a kind of assent to it. He might put laurel on his front door on some occasion of public rejoicing. But that is by association a kind of idolatry, even if it is the emperor who is honoured. 'If you have renounced temples, do not make your own gate a temple.' Then, suddenly, he becomes more sympathetic:

So far as concerns ceremonies at private and family festivals, like putting on the white toga (the sign of manhood), celebrating an engagement or a marriage, or giving a name, I am disposed to think that we are in no danger from the whiff of idolatry in them. We must take the cause of the ceremony into account.

He is alluding to celebrations in families where some are Christian and some pagan, and where, as he makes plain, a sacrifice to the family or other gods will take place. Within this relative privacy, when motives need not be misunderstood, family ties can be respected. Even so, the Christian must make distinctions. If he is invited in so many words to take part in the sacrifice, he will refuse; if that is not said, he can go, just as a spectator – a principle which Tertullian would not apply to the public shows where there was no obligation to attend and every probability of misunderstanding.

This brings him to the very difficult, and increasingly important, problem of Christians in public service. About military service he

makes the points already summarized from *De Corona*. As to
other government services, let us hear his own forceful answer:

Can a servant of God undertake an administrative office or
function if, by favour or ingenuity, he can keep himself clear of
every form of idolatry, as Joseph or Daniel, in royal purple,
governed Egypt or Babylon, performing their functions without
taint of idolatry? Grant that a man may succeed in holding his
office, whatever it may be, quite nominally, never sacrifice, never
authorize a sacrifice, never contract for sacrificial victims, never
delegate the supervision of a temple, never handle their taxes,
never give a show at his own expense or the State's, never preside
over one, never announce or order a festival, never even take an
oath; and on top of all that, in the exercise of his magisterial
authority, never try anyone on a capital charge or one involving
loss of civil status (you may tolerate inflicting a fine), never condemn to death by verdict or legislation, never put a man in irons
or in prison, never put to torture — well, if you think that is
possible, he may hold his office!

This passage (c. 17) applies most directly to men holding high
office in the State, but minor officials and humble State employees
also would find it hard to escape all compromise with pagan
religious observances. Lastly, Tertullian comes to legal instru-
ments, business contracts and the like, in which an oath was commonly required, and declares himself against the compromises
which non-Christians devised to help Christians out of the difficulty created by Jesus' words, Swear not at all. 'Let us pray to the
Lord that we may not fall into the necessity of any such contract.'
So to his peroration. No one is to say, 'Who can take enough
precautions for safety? We shall have to go out of the world.' It is
a better bargain to go out than to stay in the world an idolater.
There is no room for any trace of idolatry in the Church. We must
observe our own Christian law through which we are recognized
and put to the test by the heathen.

Tertullian's opinions are extreme, though possibly he sometimes
had his tongue in his cheek, using shock methods to stimulate the
conscience. He was a rigorist whose very occasional concessions
surprise us, and his rigorism took him into the Montanist sect of

which we shall hear elsewhere. One can see how such an outlook might encourage the common charge that Christians were enemies of the human race or, at best, useless to it. Aware of this danger, he himself tries to repel the attack in works which he hoped pagans would read, like the *Apology*, addressed to Roman magistrates. We are not exiles from life, he tells them, we do not reject the good things God has given us. We live together with you in this world, using your markets and shops and factories and inns, buying and selling, working in the fields. You can use our labour and our craft-skills. How can we be unfruitful in business? We go to sea with you, serve in the army with you. You'll find us in villages, towns and cities, in town-councils, law-courts, senate and palace. We are honest and thoroughly loyal. Though we cannot worship the Emperor, we pray for him and for the peace and welfare of the Empire.[4]

This was more or less true in fact; whether it was disingenuous of Tertullian in particular to use such arguments is another question. Many Christians could do so in good faith, since they believed some *modus vivendi* in a pagan environment could be found. If Christians lived honestly in the world, their neighbours would respect them and come to tolerate them, making allowances for their peculiar views, as in the instance of the oaths. Tertullian admits that some of the matters he raised were subjects of discussion and dispute; perhaps it was because he could not get his own way that he broke with the Church in Carthage. Evidently some felt that the Church need not irritate the world by scrupulosity in social observances, that some harmless concessions and conformities would actually fend off blasphemies against the Name, that somehow or other the Roman State must be made to see that there was room for the Christian churches within it — the line which Tertullian himself took when writing as an apologist. Others had different ideas about what constitutes worldliness, and were more frank in their acceptance of God's gifts not as a compromise with human frailty but as good in themselves. Thus while Tertullian feared pagan philosophy (or so he said), Clement of Alexandria

[4] *Apology* 42, cf. 37.

and Origen accepted its aid in their theological work, and Clement had comparatively liberal views about sex and property. It would not be easy, as time went on without the Second Coming of Christ, and Christians increased in numbers, to evade decisions about their duty in society.

If we reject some of Tertullian's scrupulosity and think him one-sided, we must acknowledge the value of his sharp probing into the Christian conscience. Essentially he is forcing not points of detail but fundamental principle. Everyday activities are ultimately controlled by some religion or ideology. What does loyalty to God in Christ demand? If we are not conscious of the assumptions which decide our daily habits, they must be brought up into consciousness. We cannot drift with the tide, which may be flowing against Christ. We must ask what is compatible with our baptismal profession, and stand against what is incompatible. The Church must be holy to God, and be seen to be holy, thereby witnessing to God in the world. Autonomies like 'business is business', 'art for art's sake', 'reasons of State', must be questioned.

Most Christians of that day were much nearer to Tertullian than to any humanist ideal. They reacted from the sexual immorality and irresponsible wealth which they saw around them; they could not see how to become fully engaged in contemporary society, and although there were long periods of practical toleration, they had no legal security against the persecution which fell upon them from time to time and which must have weeded out those more inclined to compromise. Concern for the holiness of the Church, for the sake of God and their own salvation, predominated over any hope of changing society. This, they believed, entailed separation from the world, from which, if it must be, they were willing to 'depart' by martyrdom.[5] Whether the separation should be enforced upon individual believers by some kind of Christian law, an ecclesiastical discipline involving expulsion of grave offenders from the holy community, would have to be considered. Further, the degree and nature of necessary separation might vary with cir-

[5] See W. H. C. Frend, *Martyrdom and Persecution in the Early Church* (Blackwell, 1965).

cumstances; watchfulness against ecclesiastical rigidity, perhaps against clerical conservatism, would be required, and common sense against enthusiastic extremists who could not distinguish between earth and heaven and who hived off into perfectionist sects whenever they thought the Church was compromising its holiness. I shall come to discipline and legalism and sectarianism in later chapters. Meanwhile let us be clear that in the early days of its expansion, and without feeling any contradiction between its outlook and its evangelistic duty, the Church saw its mission largely in terms of holiness and separation from the world, that is, from the thoughts and desires and customs of the majority of men and women among whom Christians lived.

IV

The same principles and similar difficulties in their detailed application are with us today, both in societies which have been strongly affected by Christianity and appear to be moving away from it, and in those to which it has come as a novelty or intrusion into a traditional way of life with quite other foundations. Always there is the interplay between principle and the concrete decisions which have to be taken according to present circumstances. So it was in the fourth century. Tertullian had seen how different it would be if Caesars could be Christians – but that was unthinkable. With Constantine it had happened, changing the outlook for the Church so completely that the meaning of holiness had to be reconsidered. Persecution gave place to toleration and imperial patronage. Opportunity for widespread evangelism brought with it the perils of nominal, socially conforming, conversions or of deceptive half-conversions in which pagan habits were syncretized with Christian teaching. Instruction, pastoral care and discipline were needed on an altogether new scale. Moreover, since magistrates and public servants were no longer compelled to partake in idolatrous ceremonies, Christians could hold office in the State and must consider whether this was now their duty, and if so how to perform it. The Church must review its positive duty to a society in which Christian institutions could now be built up. It must decide what existing institutions to fight with its new authority and backing – slavery, perhaps, or gladiatorial shows or prostitution. Must its earlier attitude to the established forms of law and government, industry and commerce, undergo a revolutionary reappraisal? Perhaps the Church should have a social and economic policy? It was a time of temptation, when high standards might drop and worldliness capture the Church. The monastic movement is proof that many believed the world had conquered the Church; they fled from both cherishing an older ideal of holiness. It was also a time of opportunity, when the more subtle temptation might be, precisely, withdrawal from the world.

I pass over the centuries and come to modern times. We often say, with truth, that the Church at home is again living in a missionary situation in which the old problems return in a new guise: relation to a science-controlled culture, possibility of new forms of syncretism, demands for moral compromises, nominal Christianity, need for instruction, anxieties about discipline, and sometimes a longing to abandon problems for the authority and tradition which provide clear answers and warm security. But our attention must be directed rather towards the so-called younger churches overseas.

V

The picture of the Victorian missionary sheltering from the sun under a tree or his umbrella and telling the story of Jesus or preaching hell-fire to a handful of curious natives is a caricature if taken to represent what he did with most of his time. He is more likely to have been busy with the administration of a mission settlement, with money, letters, buildings, food, servants, wondering how much time he can keep for spiritual work and frequently forced to exercise judicial and governmental functions. Here is an outstanding difference between early and more modern evangelistic methods. There were no separate Christian settlements in the first few centuries, and the Apologists used this fact. Christians do not live somewhere in cities of their own, said the writer of the *Letter to Diognetus*. But that is just what happened later on, if for cities we say villages. In Paraguay, early in the seventeenth century, the Jesuits collected their Indian converts into Christian villages. In China, after Ricci's policy of assimilation to Chinese culture had broken down, Catholic missionaries tried to group Christians in isolated villages, away from politics and contamination. In Java missionaries found capital for clearing the jungle, so that the growing number of Christians could farm land in newly-founded village communities. Dr Ajayi[6] tells us that in Nigeria Henry Townsend did not want mission stations to become Christian villages, which are described as a Roman Catholic device! The only settlement there which much resembled those in Paraguay was established at Topo in 1876. In the words of the Father Superior:

We admit on the land of the mission families who wish to put themselves under the rules we have imposed. They cultivate the land for their own profit except for a little rent paid in kind. Their children must be baptized and brought up in the Catholic faith. When they grow up, we see to their progress. For this reason we give them in advance a plot of land to cultivate, and when they have been sufficiently instructed to be able to live without the supervision of the mission, they get married.

When Ajayi calls Topo unique in Nigeria, it is (I take it) because it tried to be a little Christian State, with the missionaries claiming, or acting upon, various exemptions from secular control and exercising this control over their own people; and he shows how Protestants, including the Secretary of the Presbyterian Foreign Mission Committee, feared the dangerous principle which 'in the palmy days of popery' made the clergy demand exemption from the operation of the Civil Power. In the Protestant villages of Nigeria, he says, there was not much physical separateness; many emigrants and converts continued to live within the old society but were no longer part of it.

    [6] J. F. A. Ajayi, *Christian Missions in Nigeria 1841-1891* (Longmans, 1965), pp. 113-17.

However true that may be of Nigeria, it was different elsewhere in Africa. Some examples are indeed Roman Catholic. When Cardinal Lavigerie rescued starving orphans from a great famine in Algeria, he put them into orphanages which soon turned into Christian villages under the White Fathers; and this became his settled policy for Central Africa. Ransomed slave-children in self-contained villages could escape the dangers of a heathen environment and become true lights of a civilization of which the Gospel is the source and the law. Roland Oliver describes such a station. In its schools life was regulated almost as severely by the mission bell as it was in England by the factory hooter. When pupils grew up and married, they worked three days a week on the mission estate for a small wage and on three others cultivated their own plot, which the mission gave them free of charge. Free outsiders were allowed to settle on mission land on condition that they kept the rules in all their rigour and placed themselves under religious instruction. They prospered: *il fait bon vivre chez les Blancs*. But these White Fathers claimed the right to rule their people. We have full authority over them, they said, and there were conflicts with civil authority, African and European.

According to Oliver, the Scottish Presbyterians thought like the Catholics in this respect, so that their stations also developed into fully fledged economic and political units, governed and directed by the missionaries and more or less separated off from the surrounding tribes. Sometimes missionaries had to be reproved for their clumsy attempts to exercise criminal jurisdiction, with floggings and at least once a death sentence. The Anglicans (Church Missionary Society, Universities' Mission to Central Africa) and Congregationalists (London Missionary Society), though in theory disclaiming temporal authority, could not altogether avoid coercive and disciplinary severities, especially in their settlements for freed slaves.[7]

The advantages of such separated and disciplined villages are

[7] R. Oliver, *The Missionary Factor in East Africa* (Longmans, 1965). pp. 44-65.

evident: daily life can be explicitly Christian for the whole community, with worship, instruction, Christian moral standards, opportunity to grow firm in faith, free from the constraints of tribal custom. They may be wonderful places for training pastors and evangelists. On the other hand, even if political authority is abjured and paternalistic control relaxed in due course, such enclaves may be tempted to live in and for themselves, too remote from the main centres of life to have much influence over them, too alien a culture to transform indigenous society. Beginning with a promise of progress, they slip into a traditionalism of their own.

An alternative to physical separation is spiritual separation, in the world but not of it, with mission stations planted among non-Christians and converts continuing to live in their old towns or villages. Enthusiastic converts are eager to demonstrate their break with the past. One mark, of deep significance, is the new Christian name; clothing can be another, like western trousers or skirts, sometimes required by a prudish missionary, sometimes proudly worn against the missionary's wishes.[8] And while many practices must be rejected as intrinsically sinful (it is silly to shut one's eyes to the evil in paganism), some converts will choose to give up altogether what others regard as harmful only in excess. The Muruts in Borneo stopped smoking on conversion, and the Jungpaw Christians in Burma cut out beer as well as opium. It marked them off. Again, many converts who retain contact with their clan or tribe may refuse to attend ceremonies which are not wrong in themselves but may be wrong in their setting. Having made the point sufficiently through Tertullian, I need not labour the many problems posed by the call to holiness in an idolatrous

---

[8] Cf. B. Idowu, *Towards an Indigenous Church* (Oxford University Press, 1965), p. 38: 'From the beginning of Christianity in Nigeria, it has been associated with the European form of dress . . . Until very recently, there were churches which no person would dare to enter for worship on Sunday unless he is "properly dressed", that is in the European way.' Note Bishop Patteson in Melanesia: 'I must be very careful lest they should think that wearing clothes is Christianity . . . Some clothing is desirable no doubt' (*Life* by C. M. Yonge, II, pp. 253-54).

environment. 'Come out, be separate' is always a stern challenge. In J. C. Pollock's book, *Earth's Remotest End*, a Borneo Christian tells how his headman wants to say farewell to the spirits *slowly*. 'What's the good of that?' he asks. The same book dwells on the danger to Christians in the Japanese partiality for syncretism, the temptation not to discern between religion and culture, to attend Shinto festivals much as an Englishman might watch morris-dancing, a pleasant and interesting custom. 'The Church is weak,' a Japanese pastor says, 'because many churches don't preach against idolatry. Either compromise, and let your so-called be-lievers hang on to the old beliefs, or trust the Holy Spirit to break through.'[9]

That is downright, and, in so far as this is a yes-or-no matter, the right choice. But suppose it is really more complicated? Suppose the Holy Spirit has something else to say, even about culture and the relation between foreign and indigenous cultures? In the third century Origen talked of spoiling the Egyptians, getting all we can out of Greek culture for Christianity. The fourth century brought much assimilation of pagan habits, some of it useful, like 'baptizing' and moralizing festivals, some of it disputed among Christians today, like the cult of local saints. Patristic and medi-aeval thought was deeply indebted to Plato and Aristotle. Early Catholic missionaries in China tried to win the friendship of Chinese sages and scholars, and to give a Christian turn to an-cestor-worship. We are probably rather attracted today by Coolen's use of Javanese drama. Pollock speaks approvingly of a Thai Christian who set a fine hymn to an old melody from the classic plays and put another on the *Wounds of the Cross* to a tune sung by the King in old dramas as he is being deposed.[10] The Salvation Army provides more homely examples. We must go deeper. Anthropologists often attack missionaries, especially of the last century, for tearing people away from their hereditary culture.

[9] J. C. Pollock, p. 261 (Muruts), p. 105 (Jungpaws), pp. 245-46 (Borneo), p. 317 (Japan). For Japan, see R. Hammer, *Japan's Religious Ferment* (SCM Press, 1962).
[10] J. C. Pollock, op. cit., p. 169.

SCM PRESS LTD
56 Bloomsbury Street
LONDON W C 1

☐ Please send me regular mailings of your publicity material

☐ I am especially interested in books for use in schools

☐ I am especially interested in paper-covered books

☐ I should like to be sent details of the Religious Book Club

☐ I should like to be sent a free specimen copy of *Learning for Living*

Name _____ Rev., Mr, Mrs, Miss

BLOCK CAPITALS, PLEASE

Address _____

_____

_____

As I have said, we cannot be blind to objective evil in any culture, even if subjectively its bearers are blameless; and bad old customs cannot be preserved as museum pieces for the pleasure of anthropologists. But equally certainly, Christianity as such does not require the wholesale adoption of European or American customs. To destroy a close-knit social structure is a tremendous responsibility and risk, and will almost certainly be wrong if you only replace it with a vacuum or with individualism. It takes time and patience to learn what customs must be abandoned and which can be integrated with new, imported elements into a genuinely Christian society. If hereditary custom is not fully understood, with all its pressures upon the convert, there will be a breakdown of communication. Then there may be hidden contamination through misunderstanding, a secret ulcer, just as serious as any which comes from a more obvious syncretism. Probably most modern missionaries, often excellent anthropologists themselves, are aware of the issues, though there are powerful fundamentalist missions which think everything can be decided by proof-texts, and such methods get a ready hearing from the biblically-minded African.

Assimilation may contaminate. As Bishop Hollis wrote, to use the word Avatar for the Incarnation in the Tamil Nicene Creed may do more harm than good, since there can be many Avatars but only one incarnate Christ.[11] Similarly, it can be argued that the biblical sense of the Word of God was perverted by the importation into it of Greek ideas of the Logos. Yet it is a wonderful fact that the Christian faith, born in a Semitic land, was soon the religion of Greeks and Romans, and then, having become to all appearance inextricably bound up with Graeco-Roman culture, survived the shattering of the Empire to be the faith and civilizing force of Celtic and Germanic peoples. It is not tied to any one culture. It stands for the universal Lordship of Christ, and its mission is to the whole world. It cannot fulfil its mission without manifold engagement in the life of the world.

I have tried in this chapter to open up my whole subject by

[11] Michael Hollis, *Paternalism and the Church* (Oxford University Press, 1962), p. 37.

drawing attention to the insistent and persistent problems raised
by God's requirement of holiness. What does it mean to be not of
the world? Individuals can sit in armchairs discussing it.
Churches and missions have to take decisions. On many points of
daily life they may decide to go no further than teaching and
exhortation, leaving the final decision to the individual conscience.
Or they may decide that the holiness of the Church must be protected by discipline, by rules, by excommunication. Discipline
will be the subject of the third, fourth and fifth chapters. Before
these, we must look at the early Church's resources in pastoral
ministry and at some of the problems of ministry in the younger
churches today.

CHAPTER TWO

THE PATTERN OF PASTORAL MINISTRY

I

THE CHURCH is apostolic. It is always being sent on its mission to the world; that is one meaning of the word apostolic. What it takes to the world must be the real thing, the authentic faith and life communicated by Christ to his people through the Apostles; that is the other meaning of apostolic. To perform its mission, the Church must itself be living by the gifts which the Lord himself gave, and continues to give to it, as the condition and means of life in him: the Gospel, the Word of God, the sacraments, the fellowship with the mutual love and care for one another of all its members, all the truly Christian activities which the Holy Spirit inspires.

This means that, in order to build the Church up for its own inner life and its service to the world, a great diversity of things has continually to be done: worshipping God, with whatever practical arrangements that requires, preaching the Gospel, converting people, teaching children and adults the meaning of the Bible and its application to life, baptizing, joining in the Eucharist, helping individuals in body and soul, encouraging the moral witness of each congregation, maintaining whatever order and discipline enables each community to serve God best, looking after Church property and supervising the distribution of Church funds. These and other activities are what St Paul calls *diakoniai* services, ministrations, which have to be performed within the one body of the Church by its different members. And since the ability so to serve comes from the Holy Spirit, he also calls them gifts, *charismata*, and spiritual things, *pneumatika*, words which we often combine into spiritual gifts.

How can these be used to full advantage? The very fact that they are gifts of the Spirit raises a problem. For must not every Christian exercise his own ministry as the Spirit directs? And may that not mean that on the one hand he must not act unless he is aware of the Spirit's impulse, while, on the other hand, he must act if he is convinced of it? Yet it may not be sensible if we all wait to see whether anyone wishes to preach a sermon, and it will certainly not be edifying if we all rush for the pulpit the moment the time comes for one. So Paul, while he likes to dwell on the variety and richness of spiritual gifts, tells the Corinthians that these must be used decently and in order. The principle of order goes far beyond regulations necessary to ensure that a service of worship is decently conducted: that all do not speak at once. It leads us to ask whether there is an ordering, an order of value, of the gifts themselves; and we remember that Paul prefers prophecy to speaking with tongues, says, 'Be eager for the greater gifts', and puts love higher than all. The principle of order also opens up questions about authority. Take Paul's example of teachers. Christians feel the impulse to tell others of their faith and in that sense to be teachers, maybe of their own children. This may well be the duty and service of all Christians as such. But should there also be something within the Church corresponding to the trained school-teacher with a degree or a certificate, that is, with an authority or qualification to teach recognized by the community? As normal practice that seems good sense, but since the liberty and sovereignty of the Spirit of God cannot be limited by diplomas, there will be problems about authorized and unauthorized teaching in the Church. And there may be other ministrations for which it is expedient or necessary, for the sound growth of the Church, that the minister should be specified and authorized in some recognizable way.[1]

If we have gone so far, we may find ourselves asking next who can give any such authorization. Is it the community as a whole,

[1] Rom. 12; I Cor. 12-14.

or some recognized body within the whole, like a degree-granting university, or some individual, like a king or president? At this point we perceive that the authority to act for Christ must come from Christ, even if it comes through the Church and needs outward recognition by the Church. What does it mean to say with St Paul not only that God gives us spiritual activities, but also various kinds of men, that God has set some in the Church, first apostles, secondly, prophets, thirdly teachers, or that Christ gave some to be apostles, some prophets, some evangelists, some pastors and teachers? Does it mean that these, and perhaps the bishops and elders and deacons who are mentioned elsewhere in the New Testament, are set in the Church by God as its appointed officers, with precise functions and corresponding authority? Questions like this drive us back to the Gospels to ask what is implied in Jesus' choice of the Twelve and his appointment of them as Apostles, and before long the familiar theological problems about apostolic succession and ordination and the priesthood of the whole Church raise their heads.[2]

The kind of ministry which the Church of the present and the future needs, its pattern, its deployment, are not mere matters of convenience or utility. Christian expediency arises out of Christian faith. In what follows I shall be assuming that we have the warrant of Scripture for a special ministry, commissioned by Christ through ordination for special functions within the Church.

II

Let us turn to the historical facts. According to the New Testament there was at first much flexibility, so that it might be premature to speak of a pattern of ministry. When Paul tells the Corinthians to preserve good order, he makes no mention of local ministers whom in this respect they should obey, and there is a strong case for concluding that there were then no office-holders in the church at Corinth. Perhaps he had wished to allow freedom for the promptings of the Spirit, though, as founder-apostle, he

[2] I Cor. 12.28; Eph. 4.11.

kept close watch upon the consequences and expected obedience when he intervened. Elsewhere there were elders and deacons, terms which at times need mean no more than senior men and servants but which sometimes refer to ministerial offices, while the word *episkopoi*, bishops, also possibly a function-word in some instances, is the name of an office at least in the Pastoral Epistles. Whether it is there still equivalent to the office of presbyter (elder) or distinct from and already superior to it has been much discussed; I regard them as equivalent. But at Jerusalem James is more like a later bishop, and Paul uses temporary delegates like Timothy and Titus with authority over presbyters and large areas. As a variety, we have also the prophets and teachers who, it seems, guided or governed the church at Antioch for a time. Behind this flexibility and experiment stood the Apostles, a court of reference whenever necessary. The theological question for the future would be whether this apostolic authority could and should be perpetuated, and if so how; the practical question, how best to order the variety of ministries for the welfare of the Church and its mission. The theological and practical issues are of course connected.

What happened before long was the establishment of local ministries consisting of one bishop with a number of presbyters and deacons under him, together with the acceptance of the bishops collectively as, in a broad sense, the governing body of the Church universal. The bishops were soon believed to have inherited in some measure—indeed for several early theologians in a very complete measure—the authority and responsibility of the Apostles. Many later theologians would qualify this by insisting that the exact position of the Apostles in the primitive Church was essentially unrepeatable.

Here is an early example of local episcopal government. Ignatius, bishop of the great city of Antioch, is writing around AD 115 to the church at Smyrna in Asia Minor:

All of you follow the bishop, as Jesus Christ follows the Father, and the presbytery as the apostles; and reverence the deacons as the command of God. No one is to do any church business with-

The Religious Book Club

BULLETIN 178

MAY 1967

SCM Press Ltd

56 Bloomsbury Street

London, WC1

From the Editor's Desk

The Free Book

offered to all who enrol a new member during May or June is
The Glory of Man, by David Jenkins (normally 18s., to be published
later by Scribners in the USA). David Jenkins is Fellow and
Chaplain of The Queen's College, Oxford, and Canon Theologian
of Leicester Cathedral. He also serves on the Board of Directors
of the SCM Press. Many of you will have seen and read his *Guide
to the Debate about God,* published by Lutterworth last year; this
new book, the Bampton Lectures for 1966, contains some more
immensely valuable guide-lines for our thinking about what it
means to be a Christian today. It would be misleading to pretend
that it can be read quickly and easily, few books which penetrate
to the heart of Christianity can; but I am quite sure that you will
find it a book to which you will want to return again and again
and from which you will get more at each reading. (There was a
paragraph from it at the end of last month's English edition of the
Bulletin.) As an alternative, we offer *The Sociology of English
Religion,* by David Martin (normally 25s in our edition; Heinemann
Educational are publishing a paperback edition simultaneously at
half the price. English readers see back page.) Dr Martin is a
lecturer at the London School of Economics and has produced
some often startling facts and statistics about what people in
English churches do and think!

The July Book

will be by Ernest Marvin, who is a Presbyterian minister in Lockleaze, Bristol. He is co-author of the controversial Passion play *A Man Dies*, which depicted the Passion in modern dress against a background of pop music, and which proved to be an enormous success as well as arousing considerable discussion. His new book, *Odds Against*, describes his work among young people on a housing estate near Bristol, both in church and outside it. It is realistic, vivid and at times extremely funny, and even if you don't live or work on a housing estate like this it is important to know what those who do are up against.

Future Plans

I promised to write more about these in this Bulletin, but it has to go to the printer at just the wrong time. The main lines of what we want to do are quite clear, but one or two more details must be settled before I commit myself in print. So I shall have to keep you on tenterhooks again until July. Meanwhile, do keep letting us have your comments – critical or complimentary.

The Bulletin

I have been looking at a whole series of back numbers of the Bulletin and have been struck by the way in which it has gradually changed with the times. At one stage, barely a single book published by the SCM Press was mentioned and the bulk of the Bulletin was a long article with questions which study groups could use; now, we seem to use the Bulletin largely to tell you about books which might be of interest. Of course, it is always a pleasure to write about our books, and there would be something seriously wrong if we didn't feel enthusiastic about them and want to draw your attention to what you might otherwise miss. But it may well be that you think that the Bulletin could be put to better effect and that there are other things you would like to hear about. If so, again please don't hesitate to write; after all, it is of the essence of a club that there should be some two-way traffic, and I am always glad to hear what you think.

John Bowden

Dr S. L. Greenslade

 was born in Bristol in 1905, educated at Christ's Hospital and Hertford College, Oxford, and ordained in 1929. Apart from a short curacy in Leeds he has been an academic don all his life, first as a Fellow of St John's College, Oxford, and subsequently as a Divinity Professor at Durham, Cambridge and Oxford, where he has been Regius Professor of Ecclesiastical History and Canon of Christ Church since 1960. Professorially his principal concern is with the Early Church, ecclesiastically with the modern Ecumenical Movement. He has taken part in several inter-Church conversations and is a member of the Faith and Order Commission of the World Council of Churches. He likes travel, old cities, churches and houses, museums, libraries and art galleries, old books, music old and new, and most kinds of history. He is married and has two children and two grandchildren.

Dr R. P. C. Hanson writes

Dr Hanson, who is Professor of Christian Theology at Nottingham University, is an old friend of the SCM Press and has written several books which we have published. His Torch Commentary on *II Corinthians* and his *Tradition in the Early Church* are still in print. Readers may also remember his excellent RBC book on the Trinity, *God: Creator, Saviour, Spirit*.

Church history is not a subject which attracts many readers today. It is not generally thought to qualify for the magic epithet *relevant*. Professor Greenslade's book is a fine disproof of this assumption. He discusses a number of problems which have confronted both the early Church and the Church in newly-evangelized areas overseas today, comparing both the circumstances and the solutions. He does not fall into the trap of thinking that all we have to do is to discover what the early Church did and then imitate it, but neither does he dismiss the efforts of the early churchmen to cope with their problems as irrelevant. He shows both ages facing

3

difficulties which are basically identical: assimilation or rejection of pagan culture; education of men for the ministry; long or short preparation for baptism; penitential discipline; the challenge of the schismatic sect. He offers no ready-made solutions produced by history, but his discussion illuminates each subject that it touches and makes the reader feel that he has a deeper grasp of it.

Out of his wide knowledge of Patristic literature Dr Greenslade brings up vivid examples and incidents again and again. Tertullian, even the Puritan Tertullian, does not mind pagan ceremonies at a family celebration of an engagement. At Cirta in Roman North Africa in 303 one 'reader' was a schoolmaster, another a cobbler (part-time ministry?); Gregory of Tours regarded concubinage before marriage as so prevalent a practice that he could not treat it as a sin demanding penance. He has assembled a number of examples from recent missionary experience to match the material from the ancient Church, from Paraguay, Algeria, China, Nigeria, Malawi, Uganda, South India, Hong Kong, Borneo, Java, Japan and many other places. As he ranges in space all over the globe so he moves in time from the first to the eighth century and from the Reformation to the present day.

Taking out of the treasure of his extensive learning things new and old, he weaves together Christian history and Christian pastoral experience into a whole which should certainly instruct the historian and the missionary and can hardly fail to charm the common reader.

John Macquarrie

There was a period of two or three months at the end of last year when I simply had no time to read some of the new books we were publishing, and I have only just begun to catch up. One of the books which I have found very difficult indeed to put down is John Macquarrie's latest, *Principles of Christian Theology*, which appeared in January, and costs 50s (USA, Scribners). It is not a cheap book, the title is an austere one, and it is included in our *Library of Philosophy and Theology*, which may perhaps make it appear somewhat forbidding. But, on the other hand, it is a big book, of almost five hundred pages, and offers one of the best introductions to, and accounts of, the Christian faith that I have ever seen.

John Macquarrie's first book, *An Existentialist Theology*, a study of the relationship of Bultmann to Heidegger, appeared more than ten years ago in the same series. He was then a Scotsman, a minister

4

of the Church of Scotland, teaching in Glasgow. He is still a Scotsman, but he is now an Anglican priest and teaches in New York, where he is Professor of Systematic Theology at Union Theological Seminary. His first book was in many ways a specialist one, but here was someone who did not write Bultmann off as a Teutonic thinker peddling heresy, but concentrated on listening to what Bultmann had to say and explained it with pellucid clarity, suggesting that whereas one could not simply accept Bultmann's writings as they stood without qualification, he was saying something that was important and important to *us*. His next book, *The Scope of Demythologizing*, again in the same series, took the story further and again, without rushing to judgment, listened, explained and commented in the same eminently readable way.

Since then, John Macquarrie's books have been covering an increasingly wide field. His *Twentieth Century Religious Thought*, first published in 1963 and now available as a SCM Cheap Edition, provides an invaluable guide to the philosophers and theologians of the last sixty years, and illustrates the background against which the theology he wrote about earlier should be seen. Even better, though, was his collection *Studies in Christian Existentialism*, which now appears as something of a forerunner to *Principles of Christian Theology*. I was sent a copy of it to review for the *Church Times* and felt then that it was the sort of book to recommend to anyone who wanted to know what theology is all about. One could say the same thing even more of its successor. When so much confusion reigns about what theology is and how we can do it and what we ought or ought not to believe, this *magnum opus* brings order and clarity. Perhaps you will want to disagree with it – well and good, but in the very process you will learn an enormous amount. Starting with how we think about the Christian Faith and the evidence we have to go on, Dr Macquarrie deals with all the high points of Christian belief: God, the Trinity, Jesus Christ, the Holy Spirit, the last things, the Church, the ministry, the sacraments, the word, Christianity in the world. He does not neglect the realities of twentieth century life on the one hand, and angels, saints and the Virgin Mary on the other.

The Archbishop of Canterbury wrote an enthusiastic letter about the book when he read it, and a great variety of people have been telling me how useful they are finding it. Nor is this all. Last month we published another book by Dr Macquarrie, in which he discusses how it is possible for us to talk about God in language which has grown up for use in talking about the human situation, and not things which transcend that. It is called *God-Talk* (35s) (USA, Harpers) and has all the qualities of the books which have gone before it.

Finally, as if all this were not enough, John Macquarrie is editor of the *Dictionary of Christian Ethics* which we hope to publish in October. It is becoming increasingly clear that ethics is one of the most important subjects Christians have to think about, and a whole series of distinguished contributors have, under Dr Macquarrie's editorship, provided an authoritative guide and companion which will be of enormous help in showing us how to look for the right course in the complex issues in which we seem to be involved.

Best Seller

It is not very often that we sell half the edition of a book in the first week, and when we do, it usually means that the content is controversial. All the more welcome, then, that this should have happened with *Contemporary Prayers for Public Worship*, edited by Caryl Micklem and produced by a group of Congregationalist ministers (15s), and without so much as a breath of controversy! Clearly there will be differences of opinion about the style and content of the prayers, but something like this is clearly filling a deep need. Here is one from the collection:

Lord, we have heard what you said
    to the Jews and the early Christians.
Now we must talk with you
    about our hopes and fears
    for the Church and the world
    in our own time.

We think of the Church
    as your people,
    Christ's body,
    at least a foretaste of your new creation.
Some part of your purpose
    must have been realized in it.
Sometimes the lives of Christians
    do put the world to shame.
But the Church does not proclaim the Gospel so clearly
    that people are left without excuse.

We cannot be surprised
  when they do not find Christ easily through the Church.
How can this be put right?
How can your life be released in the Church
  and transform its worship and its service?
We believe in your purpose for the Church;
  help us not to be imprisoned in unbelief.
Few of us are people of great influence and responsibility,
  and we wonder how our prayers can affect the course of the
    world's life.

We cannot believe that war or tyranny or famine or sickness
  are the conditions under which you intend men to live.
And yet many have prayed for peace,
  but war has not been averted.
The tyrant falls
  only after he has caused so much misery.
Famine is still normal for most people.
Sickness still takes its toll.
We believe that these are evils to be fought,
  and yet that mankind itself is not equipped to fight them.
We need the love only you can give,
  love which is prepared for great sacrifice,
    creative thought
    and untiring patience.
Meanwhile we ask you to give strength
  to those who suffer from these evils
  and to make us alert
    to ways of making things easier for them.

Lord, you so often astonish us
  by granting requests which were only half-formed,
  by enriching our experience in unexpected ways,
  by reminding us of factors we had overlooked.
However you answer these prayers,
  may the outcome be
    that we love you more,
    understand your purpose better,
    and believe in you with greater confidence.

Not So Secular

In his *A Sociology of English Religion,* David Martin, after looking at the facts, is not quite so pessimistic about the place of the church in our society as other writers of recent times:

Finally, there are certain general points to be made about institutional practice in Britain. Most important is the striking resilience of the churches under unique pressures, accelerating social changes and the kind of rapid social movement which erodes stable institutions of any kind which do not happen to be part of the required structure of Government. The constant use of the word 'decline' needs to be set against massive exchanges of population by migration which inevitably lowers the proportion of practising Protestants. It may also be that almost the same total number of people come to church but simply appear less frequently: certainly the virtual disappearance of attendance twice on a Sunday affects the size of congregations. At any rate the important and massive fact remains that with every incentive to spend time in an alternative manner one quarter of the population is in church at least once a month. And even if one allows for some tendency to exaggerate attendance on the part of those interrogated, that fact is in itself significant.

Of course, there are crises: but these are often occasioned by a certain confusion of role amongst clergy, even a tinge of the masochism which prefers to believe that the 'worst' is happening rather than accept a fairly stationary position: maybe this has had some impact on the special difficulties of clerical recruitment since 1964. Certainly the masochistic element seemed evident when very recent declines in confirmation and baptisms were treated out of demographic context and hailed as 'signs' of the secular society. Yet if we except some mild erosion of the more conventional rites of passage and the special difficulties of non-conformists, the position seems to have been almost stationary since the war. Let it be said quite simply that in the course of a year nearly one out of every two Britons will have entered a church, not for an event in the life cycle or for a special personal or civic occasion, but for a service within the ordinary pattern of institutional religion.

Printed in Great Britain by Billing and Sons Ltd., Guildford and London out the bishop. Let that be regarded as a valid eucharist which is under the bishop or one to whom he entrusts it. Wherever the bishop appears, there let the people be; just as where Jesus is, there is the catholic church. It is not lawful to baptize or hold an *agape* (love-feast) without the bishop. Whatever he approves, that is pleasing to God, so that everything you do may be secure and valid.

In other letters Ignatius strikes the same note. Attacks upon the unity and sound faith of the local church can be warded off if the people hold closely and obediently to the ministry; within the ministry there are three definite ranks or orders: bishop, presbyter and deacon, with the bishop at the top in full control. What functions the presbyters and deacons carry out from day to day we are not yet told, nor is it said that the bishop can only entrust baptism or eucharist to them. But whatever they do and whatever the laymen do, at any rate of a formal nature, is under his direction. 'Do nothing apart from the bishop.' Though it was probably not until much later in the second century that all local churches were working to this pattern, it is beyond question that when monepiscopacy, as it was called, was generally established, it was accepted whole-heartedly in most quarters.

As time goes on and evidence accumulates we see more clearly what the bishop had to do. So far as was practicable, it was he who preached, he who baptized, he who celebrated the eucharist, he who administered ecclesiastical discipline. He ultimately controlled Church property, which was perhaps legally vested in him in days when the churches were not legal corporations. He is the teacher and shepherd of his flock, and for a century or two it is customary to refer to him alone as 'the priest' (*hiereus, sacerdos*). He appoints his presbyters and other ministers. Obedience is due to him as the head of his people. He in turn is expected to know his people individually or at least ensure that their needs are made known to him through assistant ministers.

In such a bishop one sees something like the parish priest, or minister of later times; and it was part of the meaning of *episkopos* (supervisor) that these pastoral and sacramental functions should be gathered together in his person, he having the final

B

responsibility for the care of souls in his area. But what was his area? To say that he exercised all these functions as far as practicable needs analysis, and we have to do some guessing for want of precise contemporary evidence. At first he would be bishop of a congregation rather than a territory, of the church *in* Ephesus, not of Ephesus, perhaps of all Christians nearer to his normal centre than to any other bishop's. It would soon become natural to think territorially: the bishop is responsible to God for the area round his centre. And since, in marked contrast to much subsequent missionary work, the early congregations were usually established in cities, it was sensible to have a bishop for each city. 'City' means the unit recognized by the State as an administrative unit (*polis, civitas*), with its own magistrates and council. This covered not only the built-up centre but also the surrounding country-side with its villages for a radius of ten, twenty, thirty miles according to the density of urbanization.[3]

Some cities had large populations, like Rome, Alexandria, Antioch; others, as in parts of the West or central Asia Minor, possessed many scattered villages. As Christians grew in number, the bishop must devolve some of his duties; but in order to preserve the unity of his flock, he kept a great deal in his own hands. He ordained and appointed his own clergy, who were expected to stay in the diocese all their lives – not an absolute rule, but normal practice. He himself was wedded to his diocese; translation to another see was disliked and for long rare, though opposition to it was gradually worn down on grounds of expediency. Such immobility of bishop and clergy gave a good pastor the opportunity to become a true *pastor pastorum* or Father-in-God to his clergy, though it had its disadvantages; without fresh blood they might all get into a rut. Next, he reserved baptism to himself, except in emergency. From Tertullian of Carthage and Hippolytus of Rome we learn that by AD 200 it was normally administered at Easter,

---

[3] This likening of an early bishop to a parish priest is often exaggerated. See my article, 'The Unit of Pastoral Care in the Early Church', in *Studies in Church History II*, ed. G. Cuming (Nelson, 1965), and in general for the early bishop, W. Telfer, *The Office of a Bishop* (Darton, Longman and Todd, 1962).

with Pentecost a second possibility, by the bishop himself in the cathedral. This was an important link with his people. A little later the *Didascalia*, a Syrian document, describes the bishop as the high priest 'who loosed you from your sins, regenerating you by water', and Firmilian, Bishop of Caesarea, the capital of Cappadocia, declares that authority to baptize, no less than to ordain, belongs to the bishop. He also administered the ecclesiastical discipline which I shall describe in later chapters. Excommunication and reconciliation depended on his decision, and if this gave him power which might be abused, it also afforded opportunities of spiritual counsel.

Baptisms, ordinations and formal discipline could be restricted to special occasions. What about matters which must occur every day or every week? First, it surprises many to learn that right into the fifth century bishops tended to keep for themselves the prerogative of preaching, though exceptions were allowed. Presumably this was how they felt able to discharge their duty as guardians of the true faith. In early days, at least, the bishop's chair (*cathedra*) was his teaching-chair rather than his governmental throne. Further, the bishop was the celebrant of the Holy Communion in his cathedral, to which people gathered from the villages on high festivals. Pictures of the Sunday gathering left us by Justin Martyr about the middle of the second century and Tertullian at its close suggest that villagers came in to the central church on ordinary Sundays also, so that the full fellowship might be experienced under the presidency of the one bishop through worship and teaching and pastoral care and discipline and charitable administration, all brought together.[4] A bishop might well cling to this unification of pastoral and sacramental life. Some devolution, however, became imperative. If not preaching, elementary teaching could be done by others, and so could pastoral visits, and there had to be more Sunday services.

Roughly what happened was that the deacons became a personal staff to the bishop, much occupied with financial administration and the supervision of charity, though they also had their

[4] Justin, *I Apology*, 67; Tertullian, *Apology*, 39.

particular liturgical functions, especially in the cathedral; and sometimes they worked in outlying towns and villages. There is the tantalizing instance of Sanctus, called 'the deacon from Vienne', in 177. Vienne was an important city near Lyons, and it looks as if the deacon was in charge of it, under the Bishop of Lyons. The presbyters usually lived in the main city with the bishop, acting as his council. Cyprian, though quite an autocrat in some ways, disliked taking any novel step, even in times of great emergency, without the approval of his presbyters. They could also do particular pieces of work for him as and when he wished. We know that by the third century they were sent sometimes to live in the villages, conducting services and behaving like parish priests. Yet at first they were not parish priests as we understand it. They were sent on recall, the areas were not marked, out and regularly staffed as parishes, and the clergy were much restricted, especially in that they did not baptize or administer discipline. Approximation to a parochial system was going on all the time, and this became normal in the end, roughly by the sixth century; but the pastoral unit of the early Church was the bishop's diocese, then often called *parochia*. In that area he was the minister of word and sacrament and the pastor.[5]

Problems were set by the rapid expansion of the Church from Constantine's time onwards, that is, after AD 313. Once, as we saw, the bishop had somewhat resembled the modern parish priest of a good-sized parish with a few assistant clergy; he could know most of his people individually. If that was so valuable, should episcopal units be multiplied so that none of them contained more than a few square miles and a few thousand people? Should there be several bishops in a great city, and one in every town or rural district? This was a genuine possibility which had to be considered, and we hear sometimes of bishops in comparatively small places which were not technically cities. We hear also of objections to this, objections which prevailed and can be illustrated by

[5] For Vienne, Eusebius, *Historia Ecclesiastica*, V, i. 17; for early parishes, G. W. O. Addleshaw, *The Beginnings of the Parochial System* (St Anthony's Press, n.d.).

a canon passed at the Council of Serdica (Sofia) in AD 343: permission must not be granted to ordain a bishop in any village or small city for which a presbyter is sufficient . . so that the name and authority of bishop shall not be cheapened (*ne vilescat nomen episcopi et auctoritas*). This shows (i) that presbyters were being put in charge of small places; (ii) that some people wanted to multiply bishops; (iii) that the decision went against it. The motives of the objectors may have been mixed, with episcopal pride and vested interest playing some part and ambitious presbyters in the other camp. Better motives might include the belief through experience that within a diocese a bishop, in order to do his work as Father-in-God, needs to be a man of special ability and personal weight, supported by the authority which goes with high responsibility; secondly, that if the bishops are to be collectively the governing body of the whole Church, meeting in regional or general councils for that purpose, they must come as men with considerable pastoral and administrative experience and must, each of them, represent something substantial in the Church; and thirdly that if bishops are to play a useful part in the social life of the Empire, now that conditions allow it, they must be men of some eminence. There were dangers here of ambition for power or wealth, of prelacy; rightly or wrongly, this was the decision, and, though it took time, the norm of one city, one bishop, was accepted. The emperor Zeno (474-491) made it, with certain exceptions, the law of the State.

With this settled, we can go back to the pattern of ministry within the diocese, and watch the play between fixity and flexibility. The fixed elements, regarded as theologically sanctioned or demanded, and not simply as expedient, were the distinction between clergy and laity, the distribution of the clerical order into three major grades, bishop, presbyter and deacon, the requirement that each minister should be regularly ordained to his functions, and the definition of some of those functions. In particular, the bishop alone was believed to have the right and power to ordain, and bishops and presbyters alone to have the right and power to celebrate the eucharist, and these two grades or orders were held to possess *sacerdotium*, priesthood. All this had come to be accepted, rightly or wrongly, as the given structure of the Church. Beyond that, flexibility was actually facilitated by the high authority of the bishop in a sizeable diocese and by the absence of a developed parochial system. In regular parishes the duties of the clergy are more or less uniform, and each man has to make the best of his talents, doing some things for which he is not particularly suited and restricted about some things he could do well. In the early diocese some presbyters could live in the city, and of those some could be given specialist functions, like cathedral canons today, while others looked after the city congregations; others could be sent on evangelistic or pastoral missions, short or long, in the countryside, the bishop moving them as he thought fit. The deacons were available for various administrative duties and were often specialists. Some would go on to the presbyterate, but many stayed deacons, their order or office being recognized as distinct and valuable in itself, not a brief preparation for a higher grade. For example, the deacon Paulinus was secretary to Ambrose, Bishop of Milan, and the Roman deacons, limited to the traditional seven, were at one time responsible for the administration of one region of Rome each, and later they or the subdeacons might be employed in supervising the revenues of the vast estates which the See of Rome possessed in Italy and Sicily. Deacons were also used as messengers, handling delicate negotiations between churches; the papal representatives at Constantinople were usually Roman deacons, like Gregory the Great before he became Pope.

Below the deacons were clerics in minor orders, which were not uniform throughout the Church. There would be subdeacons to assist the deacons and readers, commonly boys or young men being prepared for full ordination, who read the lessons in services. There might also be acolytes and exorcists, while even the door-keepers were sometimes counted as clerics. We happen to have the Roman clergy list of AD 251: 1 bishop, 46 presbyters, 7 deacons, 7 subdeacons, 42 acolytes, with 52 exorcists, readers and door-keepers. Soon large cities would have far more clergy; in

451 the diocese of Edessa had over 200 of whom 14 presbyters, 37 deacons, 23 subdeacons and 1 reader were attached to the cathedral church. But figures are sadly rare and we never know the distribution of ministers over the diocese.

At the other end of the scale the bishop was free to experiment with superior administrators. The archdeacon, first mentioned by that name at Carthage in 303, was of high importance and often succeeded his bishop; for some centuries he really was the chief deacon, in deacon's not priest's orders. An experiment which might have altered the pastoral pattern considerably was in the use of country-bishops (*chorepiskopoi*), men in episcopal orders charged with pastoral care of part of the diocese but subordinate to the diocesan. St Basil had fifty of them in his large diocese of Caesarea. But the experiment, which we hear of mostly in the East during the fourth century, proved unpopular. In practice the relation between diocesan and assistant could be awkward, while in theory the assistant, like the modern Anglican suffragan bishop, does not fit easily into the full theological picture of the bishop as responsible Father-in-God and centre of unity, as one soon finds when trying to expound episcopacy to non-episcopalians. So instead, though somewhat later, rural deans were set over groups of parishes. All these were offices, not orders: the *chorepiskopos* was a bishop, the archdeacon a deacon or presbyter, the rural dean a presbyter. Similarly it was thought expedient to group dioceses into provinces, usually accepting the civil province of the empire as the unit, each presided over by a metropolitan or primate who gradually acquired considerable powers by custom and canon law; but in order he was still a bishop, and when the great patriarchates which grouped provinces together came into existence, their heads were still by order simply bishops, although some theological claims were made about their status, most obviously for the Bishop of Rome. But we are not concerned here with these higher forms of administration.

I have emphasized the possibilities of flexibility in the early diocese. Not that the parochial system was a mistake when it came, since provision had to be made for direct pastoral care as the Church expanded and entered into different social conditions such as those of the German tribes. But the territorial parish with an incumbent and a curate or two and perhaps a few people corresponding roughly to the minor orders is not, theologically speaking, a fixed or given element in the structure of the Church. The worshipping congregation is a constitutive element, and it needs a ministry of word and sacrament; but whether the over-all administration and the over-all pattern of ministry should be parochial or something else is a matter of sanctified expediency.

III

For some minds the early Church itself became too institutional and too clerical, not only after Constantine but already in the second and third centuries. Tertullian satirizes the ministerial arrangements of unorthodox groups:

> You can't tell which is a catechumen, and which a full member. They ordain capriciously, at random. Sometimes they appoint novices, sometimes secular officials, sometimes renegades from us. Nowhere is promotion easier than in the rebel camp, since the mere fact of being there deserves a reward. So one man is bishop today, another tomorrow. Somebody can be a deacon today, but only a reader tomorrow, or a presbyter today and a layman tomorrow. For they let laymen perform priestly duties. As for their women, they are a forward lot, with the impudence to teach and argue, perform exorcisms, promise cures — perhaps even to baptize.[6]

When he wrote this soon after AD 200, Tertullian was a strong advocate of order and discipline, arguing like Irenaeus of Lyons that the true Church could be identified by its bishops in regular succession from the Apostles: they were testimony to and organs of the historic continuity, and with it the authentic Christian tradition, of each local church. Some at least of the nonconformist bodies had different ideas about the relative values of order and freedom, and ten years later this fiery satirist had thrown in his

---

[6] Tertullian, *De Praescriptione Haereticorum* 41 — a free translation with some rearrangement of sentences.

lot with one of them, the Montanists. He was moved chiefly by the desire for a more ascetic and, in the moral sense, more disciplined life than the Catholic Church demanded. It could be lived, he believed, through uninhibited response to the immediate direction of the Holy Spirit. Not that he ever disregarded the Bible; but it was a tenet of the Montanists that the Spirit speaking through prophets, rather than the established clergy teaching through tradition, would open the Bible and all revelation to them. Montanist enthusiasm had its dangers and absurdities, to be sure, but it was a fair point to ask what had happened to the prophets whom, according to Paul, God had set in the Church next after the apostles. Did they belong, as many say of the apostles, only to the founding-fathers of the Church, or should they be a permanent element in its ministry, and if so, how? In Old Testament times it had never been easy to fit the prophets into a regular pattern of ministry, and false prophets were a problem. So too in the Church. The *Didache*, dating probably from about AD 100, shows how delicate it was to apply tests to a prophet without blasphemy against the Holy Spirit:

Any prophet speaking in the Spirit you shall not try or test . . . This sin shall not be forgiven. Yet not everyone that speaks in the spirit is a prophet, but only if he has the ways of the Lord. From his ways therefore the false prophet and the prophet shall be recognized.

The Lord does raise up prophets, to whom we should listen. If they are content to give their message and leave its acceptance to the general Christian mind and conscience, there may be no great difficulty. The problem is their authority in relation to recognized authority. Do they come as interventions from heaven with over-riding authority? In fact we hear less and less of prophets as time goes on, presumably in reaction from Montanist insistence upon them.[7]

There was and is a similar difficulty about teachers. Although in the New Testament the word may often refer to a function exercised by a pastor or presbyter, it seems sometimes to denote

[7] For Montanism, see also pp. 79, 109-10, 119-20.

a particular office. What authority has an able theologian who is not ordained? On what conditions may lay teachers set up schools? Officially, on early Church theory, the guardian of orthodoxy is the bishop. Can he therefore contradict or suppress the views of learned men with whose studies he cannot keep up, for lack of ability or time? Is the bishop guarded from any false step by his understanding of Christian tradition or by some *ex officio* gift of the Holy Spirit?

IV

A few things remain to be said about the early ministry. First, it quickly became indigenous. The Apostles and other eminent missionaries went their way, leaving behind them a ministry of local men; the prophets of whom the *Didache* tells were also itinerant, and many of the teachers. If any of these settled down, they might become bishops or other ministers of their place of residence, but their successors would largely be local men, very soon. The unity of the Roman Empire and the relative unity of its culture made this possible. Missionaries rarely arrived as bearers of cultural and technological enlightenment or as literates to illiterates; they might be inferior in education. Language problems were slight: in cities you could talk to almost anyone in the Greek or Latin in which you and he had been brought up. The essential Christian doctrines could be imparted fairly quickly, Christian ways of worship demonstrated, ethical demands explained in principle, Christian books given for copying in the original tongue. There were many exceptions to my sweeping generalization. When the faith was taken to the Latin West it was organized into churches most easily where there were Jewish synagogues to help with their similar faith, or among Greek communities in the great cities. In Rome Christianity was Greek, for some time, producing its literature in Greek, worshipping in Greek, having bishops with Greek names. Tertullian sometimes wrote for Carthaginian Christians in Greek. Irenaeus, Bishop of Lyons, was a Greek from Asia Minor, and his only known prede-

cessor as bishop bears a Greek name. There was a linguistic
problem, until the Bible had been translated into Latin and a Latin
theological vocabulary suitable for Christian ideas had been constructed. But this did not take long, since the Greeks concerned
were mainly permanent residents in the West and plenty of Latins
knew some Greek. There were more serious problems in country
areas, among the Celts in Gaul, the Berbers in Africa, the peoples
of central Asia Minor, the Copts of Egypt, and in fringe countries
like Armenia and Ethiopia. How these were overcome is part of
the grand epic of evangelization which I do not forget. But
broadly, in contrast to most modern missions, what I have said is
true. The local church could quickly carry on, provided it did not
isolate itself from the common stream of Christianity around it.

Next, the local ministers were chosen by the people, at least in
part. Clement of Rome, about AD 95, speaks of ministers appointed 'with the consent of the whole church': the whole local
church. Cyprian of Carthage, in the 250s, says expressly that the
bishop should be chosen in the presence of the people and ap-
proved as worthy by their judgment and testimony, and that
bishops should be ordained in their presence, so that the ordination, examined by the suffrage and judgment of all, may be just
and legitimate. Cyprian inferred, dangerously no doubt, from the
people's responsibility in the choice of their bishop an equivalent
responsibility to break from him if he proved unworthy. The
people's part was gradually whittled away, it is true, but sometimes they asserted it strongly, as in the familiar story of Ambrose
of Milan. About the calibre of the men chosen there is insufficient
information. It is unlikely that the general run of presbyters were
highly educated – one reason, perhaps, why they did not normally
preach. They must rather be men of character, piety and good
sense. Even bishops need not be learned, though they must be apt
to teach the traditional faith and discipline.[8]

Next, the local ministries were relatively independent, at least in
contrast with the dependence of many later congregations or

[8] I Clement, 44; Cyprian, *Ep.* 67; for Ambrose, Theodoret, *Hist.
Ecc.* IV, 7.

dioceses, upon the missionary coming from outside or the missionary society or the missions board of a distant church. Ties of affection with a mother-church might linger, and mother-churches sometimes made the most of them, even claiming rights of supervision or jurisdiction, perhaps as a court of appeal. In building up its primacy, Rome added its rights as mother-church of much of the West to what it claimed on scriptural grounds. Armenia was content for a century or so to acknowledge its dependence upon Cappadocia, from which it had been evangelized, and Ethiopia upon Alexandria, from which it continued to receive its chief bishop. When the Council of Nicaea, in 325, provided for a regular system of provinces under metropolitans, it had also to confirm the customary privileges (meaning special authority) of certain great sees, among which Rome, Alexandria and Antioch are named. But this kind of dependence differs widely from direct control by missionaries. Within the diocese the presbyters and deacons were responsible to the bishop, who was independent in his day-to-day work and otherwise responsible to a council of his fellow-bishops.

Finally, early ministers were not wholly professional and full time, and not always entirely dependent upon their ecclesiastical stipends. As so often, the evidence is insufficient and confusing. No one doubts that those in minor orders frequently earned their own living. At Cirta (Constantine in Algeria) in AD 303, one reader was a schoolmaster, another a cobbler. There are inscriptions running from the third to the fifth centuries, and from Rome to Cilicia, which commemorate presbyters who were also physician, silversmith, potter and goldsmith. In Cyprus Bishop Spiridon fed his sheep, in Syria Bishop Zeno wove linen to earn money for himself and others. After all, apostles had continued with their fishing and Paul with his tent-making. On the other hand, the labourer is worthy of his hire, and it was not disputed that the clergy might properly live from the offerings of the faithful. A common practice was to divide church revenues into four equal parts, one for the bishop's expenses, one for the rest of the clergy, one for the poor, the last for the maintenance of church buildings.

Cyprian mentions the monthly payments to presbyters. And some, including Cyprian, held strongly that the higher clergy, bishop, priest and deacon, should be whole-time and fully maintained, set free from the moral dangers and the time-consuming demands of worldly business. Evidently there were differences of theory and practice. It is not easy to decide whether the sterner view was determined by concern for pastoral expediency or for the dedicated and separated life which is sometimes called the priestly life.[9]

V

As we approach the modern situation in the younger churches, we in the West come to it, whether we like it or not, through the Reformation, when many broke away from what earlier centuries had believed to be settled and binding. Some distinguished sharply between the spheres of Faith (or doctrine) and Order, concluding that the latter is a matter of expediency in which the Church — even the local church — is entirely free to do what it thinks best; hence some new forms of ministry. Others questioned the necessity of particular forms (apostolic succession or the threefold ministry) and canvassed the implications of the priesthood of the whole Church for lay ministries; others, especially Calvinists looking to the Bible not for liberty but for authority, found there a different pattern of ministry with the emphasis upon the local pastor or minister of word and sacrament and a new place for teachers and elders. So a profusion of ideas and patterns has been taken to the younger churches.

At home, while the ecumenical movement has stimulated thought on the theological issues, practical problems have been raised by considerations of evangelism and pastoral care. If we are to have bishops, how can their authority be made constitu-

---

[9] On the payment of clergy see W. G. B. Ream in *The International Review of Missions*, 1956, pp. 420 ff. (to whom I am indebted for some illustrations, though I do not accept all his conclusions); L. Vischer in *New Forms of Ministry*, ed. D. M. Paton (Edinburgh House Press, 1965), pp. 36 ff.; and W. Telfer, op. cit., chap. 9.

tional, and how can they be relieved from the burden of administration so as to be true pastors? What is the optimum size of a
diocese in modern conditions? Should most ministers work on a
parochial basis still? Should they be grouped in teams? Should
more of them have a functional ministry, working within in-
dustries, colleges and so forth? Need all clergy be fully professional and whole-time? What educational standards should be
required of part-timers? Is leadership in worship, e.g. in the
eucharist, necessarily connected with pastoral responsibility? How
should churches use deacons and elders and lay preachers? What
can each take into its own system? And there is the controversial
question of the ministry of women.

The younger churches have all these problems with more in
addition, of which the first is the adequate provision of an indigenous or native ministry. That this could happen quickly in
the early Church was a great strength to it; if not always easy, it
was facilitated rather than hindered by cultural factors. In more
recent times the reverse has often been true; and one must have
some sympathy with missionaries who hesitated to sanction hasty
ordinations of men with little education or Christian experience,
although, to take but one example of a more confident outlook,
Henry Venn had pressed it upon the Church Missionary Society
in 1851 that the ultimate object of a Mission, under its ecclesiastical aspect, is 'the settlement of a Native Church under Native
Pastors upon a self-supporting system'.[10]

Much must depend on circumstances. Dr J. V. Taylor compares
Nyasaland and Northern Rhodesia.[11] In the former, a compact
country with a fairly concentrated population, where mission
stations and sub-stations were close together, an African could be
given charge of a sub-station without being left isolated and
unsupervised for months, so that it was practicable to ordain them
quite early in the history of the Scottish and Anglican Missions

[10] E. Stock, *History of the Church Missionary Society*, II, p. 415
(CMS, 1899).
[11] J. V. Taylor and D. Lehmann, *Christians of the Copperbelt* (SCM
Press, 1961), pp. 20-22.

there. But in Northern Rhodesia, where sub-stations were too far apart for regular supervision, it seemed better to use unordained itinerant workers, the missionary at the main station retaining close control. The London Missionary Society began work there in 1877 but produced its first three indigenous ministers in 1938. In West Africa it had proved possible to build up an indigenous ministry from an early date. Some might be cautious. Townsend, whom Venn much admired, could write to him in 1851: 'I have a great doubt of young black clergymen. They want years of experience to give stability to their characters; we would rather have them as schoolmasters and catechists.'[12] But movement towards Venn's view was quite rapid, particularly in accepting the principle that pastoral work must be done essentially by native ministers. Roman Catholics and Methodists agreed, and today it is a matter of course. Ordained Africans greatly outnumber ordained missionaries in Africa; in India the ministry is mostly Indian; and there are countries where western missionaries cannot hold office in the Church. National and political considerations have reinforced what is primarily a religious necessity.

It is not enough for the ministry to be indigenous; it must also become responsible, and here progress has been slower. Essentially it is the whole local church (of whatever region is expedient) which should carry such responsibility and autonomy as is proper in due relation to the Church universal. Within it, the local ministers must take much responsibility, not as a right, in the political sense, but as something necessary to their growth into Christian manhood. It is now generally acknowledged that these churches and their ministers should progressively be freed from the control of the missionary and the missionary society; the difficulty is to apply the principle. We come up against the paternalism of the missionary, attacked by Bishop Hollis in his *Paternalism and the Church*.[13] Paternal care of new missions, even

---

[12] Quoted from J. F. A. Ajayi, *Christian Missions in Nigeria 1841-1891* (Longman, 1965), p. 181; all his chapter 6 is relevant.
[13] Michael Hollis, *Paternalism and the Church* (Oxford University Press, 1962). See also B. Idowu, *Towards an Indigenous Church* (Oxford University Press, 1965), pp. 54-56.

with paternal discipline, has been inevitable and right; under-
standably many missionaries have been cautious in devolving
responsibility and authority, and many converts have, out of
gratitude and modesty, been slow to accept authority, have remained too docile, leaned too much upon their missionaries.
Often it may have been the docile ones who were chosen for a
limited authority which they could be trusted not to strain. But if
a church is to develop healthily, men must be trained to accept
real responsibility and exercise it in some relation to the principles
of authority natural to the society in which they live.

This may not always be democratic. Dr Sundkler and Dr Taylor
have shown how missionaries and, later, native ministers came in
some areas (Uganda is an example) to hold a position analogous
to that of a local chief, working closely with the chief himself.[14]
Since there could be few such men, this analogy is not stable
ground for the authority of a minister as such when ministers
must increase greatly in number. Moreover the institution of
chiefdom is under pressure. What is now emerging in many parts
of the world is a valuable kind of paternalism compatible with
freedom and responsibility in ministry and people—the transformation of the office of bishop into a thoroughly pastoral one,
with emphasis upon his being Father-in-God to his clergy as well
as a centre of unity. This the younger churches are free to
develop to the ultimate benefit of the West, and their increasing
interest in episcopacy is significant.

Since such bishops will promote rather than discourage ministerial responsibility, and since also ministers must be multiplied,
what are to be the qualifications for ordination with responsibility? Education? This has been so in many parts of Asia and
Africa, when the missionary brought the education, ran the
schools, and picked out good pupils for the ministry. Now, however, with more government education and a multitude of well-
paid jobs available to everyone with secondary education, many

[14] B. Sundkler, *The Christian Ministry in Africa* (SCM Press, 1962),
pp. 52-55; J. V. Taylor, *The Growth of the Church in Buganda* (SCM
Press, 1958), see index under *chiefs*.

ordained ministers are less well educated than the young people in their congregations; they have been left behind by their own pupils. This is a challenge to the able young Christian to offer himself for the ministry; but it is quite unrealistic to suppose that when a society accepts the Christian faith, it at once becomes wholly altruistic. To get an educated ministry, not only must the education be available, but there must also be for its product a reasonable status in terms of maintenance (not always easy to secure) and, even more, in responsibility, in the right to take decisions individually and corporately.

Many African and Asiatic ministers are taking great responsibilities, and literature which suggests otherwise is rapidly getting out of date. In episcopal churches, many are bishops; and in some such churches the episcopate is wholly or almost wholly indigenous. In all churches the ordained ministers, just because they are few, are exercising a supervision over groups of parishes and of unordained ministers which, with certain limitations, resembles the work of a bishop. In 1964 the Church of South India had 975 presbyters and 154 deacons for 8126 congregations. In a typical Buganda parish, thirty-four square miles, 5000 people, all church work came under an unordained parish catechist; the nearest ordained minister lived seven miles away and had charge of five parishes, about the average number. It is a widely attested experience that the able minister is soon carried off to higher administrative posts or to special forms of ministry.[15]

There must be more ordained ministers, and well-educated ones, able to deal with educated people, with urban societies, with social problems, and able to think theologically and take responsible decisions in the higher councils of their church. Meanwhile much of the day-to-day pastoral work is done by teachers

[15] For S. India, Mark Gibbard, *Unity is not enough* (Mowbray, 1965), p. 29; for Buganda, J. V. Taylor, op. cit., chap. 6, and his booklet, *Processes of Growth in an African Church* (SCM Press, 1958), p. 18. *New Forms*, p. 86, quotes a recent statement that the average Anglican priest in Kenya or Central Tanganyika would have twenty to twenty-five churches. These are averages. Fr. Gibbard met a presbyter of C.S.I. with fifty-four villages (op. cit., p. 30).

acting simultaneously as evangelists and by village catechists. But teachers change with a changing educational system; they can no longer be counted on in bulk for church work, though many do it. The catechists, very numerous, are poorly paid and poorly educated: they cannot take the responsibility necessary for a responsible church, much as the church is indebted to them. In most cases the older type of catechist was not expected to rise further, certainly not to ordination and responsible office. Speaking of Uganda Dr Taylor mentions the economic difficulties of the catechist which leave him little time for visiting, and continues:

The old-style catechist is passing from the scene. . . . There is also a new styled catechist coming on to the scene – youngsters from the junior secondary schools, trained in English, potential ordinands of the future; but the majority of the clergy do not yet know how to use such material, which contradicts the whole concept of maturity and authority in traditional Kiganda society.

'The old system of teacher-catechists in the villages has largely broken down,' says Father Gibbard reporting on South India.[16]

All this – the dwindling of the foreign missionary in numbers and in authority, the immediate shortage of educated men available for the ordained ministry in many areas, the inadequacy of the older types of unordained catechist – compels new thought about the forms of ministry. What changes are expedient for the mission of the Church, and are we theologically free to make them? This chapter is not concerned with the ministry of the laity, crucial as that is, but with the ordained ministry. What is being discussed in England with interest but something less than urgency is vital to the younger churches. From all quarters comes news of experiment. One controversial issue is the ordination of presbyters at a lower educational level than has previously been demanded, majority opinion appearing to favour this in order to meet the exigencies of pastoral care and regular administration of the sacraments, provided that efforts to obtain a well-educated ministry are not therefore relaxed. Another experiment – and

[16] J. V. Taylor, *Processes*, p. 19; Mark Gibbard, op. cit., p. 34.

surely a most promising one – has been in the ordination of men already distinguished in some secular work to be part-time ministers. In Portugal, Dr Luis Pereira was simultaneously superintendent of his local hospital and pastor to a number of small congregations in the neighbourhood before he became Bishop of the Lusitanian Church, while in Hong Kong James Chang Ling Wong, superintending engineer of a great maritime firm, was for twenty years an auxiliary clergyman until he too became a bishop. Are such men merely stop-gaps until the ministry can be filled more adequately with whole-time men who have been put through a more conventional training? Some may think so, since the relation between part-time ministers (especially if they are handpicked men) and the normal pastoral organization has its problems. But this should not be assumed. Rather, we need to be alert to new possibilities in the over-all pattern of ministry, first brought to notice by immediate circumstances and necessities but proved thereby to be of permanent value to the Church. The diaconate also is everywhere under fresh scrutiny, both in churches which use it as a brief stage before the priesthood and in those which use it as an administrative lay office. It is inherently capable of development in many ways.[17]

All this means freedom; the past is a guide, not a fetter. But how far may freedom go, under pressure of the Spirit? Mark the vitality of movements led by men under the title of prophet, recalling the early Church. They are widespread and full of evangelistic zeal. Though, like the Bantu Prophet movements studied by Sundkler,[18] they may have racial and cultural grounds, they can also be genuine attempts to embody that spiritual drive which is not necessarily allied to education or compatible with administrative prudence and responsibility. Although they often become clericalist in that complete obedience to the Prophet is

[17] Consult *New Forms of Ministry* for further information, discussion of principles, and bibliography. Also M. Gibbard, op. cit., chap. III. For a summary of similar discussions in Britain see *The Shape of the Ministry (British Council of Churches*, 1965).
[18] B. Sundkler, *Bantu Prophets in South Africa*, 2nd ed. (Oxford University Press, 1961), and cf. chap. VI of the present book.

demanded, they may be a warning against rigidity in ecclesiastical organization. However, freedom is abused if it shatters the unity of the Church into a multitude of independent sects, each believing itself to be self-sufficient through the immediate action of the Spirit, free from history, free from the considered experience and theology of the older Church. Freedom and order can both be pushed to barren extremes; the tension between them can be creative. Since the solution is not easy, the temper in which it is sought is all-important. Older and younger churches must strive to understand one another, and, in both, those whose minds tend naturally towards order must sympathize with those who naturally tend to freedom, and *vice versa*, all being ready to test every institution, old and new, in the light of the unity of the Church as well as of its pastoral and evangelistic mission. For unity and mission, we are painfully learning, are inseparable.

CHAPTER THREE

PRE-BAPTISMAL DISCIPLINE AND THE CATECHUMENATE

ON CHRISTMAS Day 597, ten thousand of the English were baptized in Kent — so Pope Gregory told the Patriarch of Alexandria. At any rate something happened on a grand scale. Bede tells how, thirty years later, Edwin of Northumbria with all the nobility and many of the commons received the washing of regeneration. Mass conversions had occurred before in tribal societies, as when Clovis and his Franks accepted baptism, and in our own day there have been mass movements in South India and elsewhere, full of promise, but quite as full of problems. The community moves as a whole, sometimes at the bidding of the king or other leader. How many, we ask, have understood, have truly been converted? Is the motive some social or economic advantage? What sacrifices will they make for Christ? How can the Church instruct them and give them pastoral care through a handful of missionaries?

Such movements could not take place in the first two or three centuries since, humanly speaking, there was no chance of converting whole areas or peoples in the more or less individualistic cities of the Roman Empire where missionaries mostly worked. They had to think of individuals or small groups like the family: save that soul, fetch him out of his society into a new one, out of the world into the Church. They could not help thinking in terms of what later theologians call the gathered congregation. How difficult it was to free people from the ties of their existing social life we have already seen. Now we must consider the process of making them members of the new society, the Church.

A modern baptismal register contains a column for the rank or profession of the father. In the first ages of Christianity, when adult or convert baptism was the rule, it was most important to ask a man his occupation since the first requirement for taking him on as a Christian might be that he should give it up. In time the questions put to inquirers were shaped up into a common pattern, though there was no absolute rule. Roman practice around AD 200 is known from the *Apostolic Tradition* of Hippolytus. First, he says, those who want to hear the word are brought before the teachers (doctors) and asked why they come to the faith (this is to find out whether they come entirely of their own will). Then the sponsors who introduce them must say whether they think the candidates should be accepted. Then they are examined touching their life. This does not mean, to see if they are already morally good. There are three questions about their condition in life. First, are they slaves? If so, and if the master is a Christian, he must consent and give a testimonial of good character; if the master is a pagan, the slave must understand that he will have to please his master – he will not get free from him, or duty to him, by becoming a Christian. Second, are they married? If so, the married couple must accept from the start the Christian view of marriage. An unmarried man must agree to live chastely or get married. Third, surprisingly, are they in their right mind? Anyone out of his mind, having a devil, must be cured before admission to hear the word. Then come the questions about occupations, some of which are impossible not only for the baptized, but for those under instruction for baptism. To abandon them will be a first test of sincerity and understanding.

Some occupations are rejected on the score of their immorality : the brothel-keeper, the prostitute, the paid homosexual must stop, or be rejected. A man with a concubine must give her up or get legally married. A slave-concubine, however, who has brought up her children well and is faithful to her master, can be accepted. (This may be relevant to the modern problem of polygamy.) But most of the difficulties relate to idolatry. Naturally a pagan priest must stop; so must a temple-guardian. Painters and sculptors must give up making idols. Astrologers, diviners, amulet-makers and the like must stop: no one who is practising any kind of magic can be admitted, and it is no good bringing him even for an interview. There are also occupations which may combine immorality and idolatry: the actor or other showman, the games-charioteer and everyone connected with gladiatorial shows. A man already an ordinary soldier can continue, provided he refuses to kill, when so ordered, and does not take the military oath (he will hardly remain long in the army on those terms), but a high officer or a magistrate will have to abandon his office. To the schoolmaster Hippolytus is merciful. Better if he gives up, but if he has no other skill he can continue.[1]

These prohibitions agree pretty well with the line taken by Tertullian, though he did not relate his strictures specifically to this preliminary inquiry. Both Hippolytus and Tertullian were rigorists. The general outlook may have been somewhat – though not greatly – easier. Changes naturally came in the fourth century when, for instance, magistrate and schoolmaster could escape idolatry and when, as most judged, it was no longer incumbent upon a Christian to refuse military service.

If these tests were passed, the inquirer was admitted formally and solemnly, with prayer and imposition of hands, into the class or order of catechumen, 'under instruction'. It was probably round about AD 200 that the catechumenate took shape as a regular institution with rules for admission, instruction and discipline preparatory to baptism. The catechumen might learn much at home, but for formal instruction he went to church. On Sundays and Festivals he was allowed to stay for the first part of the eucharist only; he listened to the readings from Scripture, including the liturgical Gospel, and to the sermon and then was sent away with a special prayer and blessing: the so-called *Missa Catechumenorum*. Besides this there were special classes taught

---

[1] The *Apostolic Tradition* is short, so I usually dispense with chapter references here. There is an English translation by Gregory Dix (SPCK, 1937), and a more critical study, with French translation, by B. Botte (Münster, 1963).

by catechists (*doctores audientium*), perhaps usually presbyters (we hear of *presbyteri doctores*) but sometimes laymen, with a reader at hand to help. We must not assume a fixed pattern. How long these preliminary classes went on is not known. They provided elementary instruction in Christian morals – the kind of thing we see in the 'Two Ways' part of the *Didache* – and in doctrine, and ensured some knowledge of the Bible.

Surviving illustrations of catechetical instruction mainly concern the second stage when more intense teaching was given for a few weeks before baptism at Easter. This was a great step forward which could not be taken hastily or without official approval, at least in the early centuries when the catechumenate lasted a long time: three years according to Hippolytus and others, two by the canons of the Spanish Council of Elvira, c. 306. Practice varied, and these were norms rather than absolute rules, from which the bishop could dispense for good pastoral reasons, a liberty one is glad to see. Even Hippolytus, who lays down the three-year period, qualifies it by saying that when an earnest candidate applies himself, conduct not time will be the judge, while Origen urges catechumens to shorten their probation by good behaviour. But the period was normally long. During it they were watched, with the emphasis on morals rather than instruction. 'Some are appointed,' Origen says, 'to inquire into the lives and conduct of those who want to join the community in order to prevent secret sinners from coming to their common gathering; those who do not commit secret sin they whole-heartedly receive and make them better every day.' When the time for final instruction arrived (to return to Hippolytus) their lives were examined. Have they lived honourably? Have they honoured widows, visited the sick, done good works while they were catechumens? Their sponsors must give testimony, and if this was favourable the candidates entered on an intensive short course of instruction in the Creed and the sacramental mysteries, accompanied by the discipline of fasting and penitential exercises and marked by appropriate ceremonies, including exorcism by the bishop. And so to baptism, which was elaborate, solemn, embedded in a great act of corporate worship, and performed in the cathedral by the bishop as chief pastor. It included what many now call confirmation, and with immediate participation in Holy Communion constituted full initiation into full membership of the Church.[2]

We see that in the third century the catechumenate was taken very seriously, though our knowledge of the detail is fragmentary as regards instruction, discipline and ritual alike. When we reach the fourth we have more evidence, but the situation has changed, and goes on changing as Christianity becomes the religion of the Empire. There are far more Christians, but the selective agencies of persecution are gone, and they are not hand-picked. It is more difficult to maintain moral standards and there is clamant need for serious instruction. On the other hand, general knowledge of Christianity is more widespread, elementary teaching can be given at home, and a long catechumenate might seem unnecessary. If it was to be quite ordinary to be a Christian, why fuss about the early stages? One consequence was more baptism of infants, and this removes instruction and moral training to the sphere of the discipline of full members, which I discuss later. But there was a contrary consequence. Earlier, most catechumens were eager for baptism and bishops had to decide when to relax the long training in response to their zeal. In the fourth century we find bishops exhorting them to make up their minds and offer themselves at long last for baptism. At Milan Ambrose used to invite catechumens during the Epiphany season to enter their names for baptism at Easter. Invite is too mild a word for Augustine at Hippo: he pleads eloquently with them:

See, it is Easter. Put your names down for baptism. . . . Knock and it shall be opened to you. I too stand here and knock. Open to me. While I speak to your ears, I am knocking at your hearts.

---

[2] Hippolytus, *Apostolic Tradition*, 16-20; cf. Tertullian, *On Baptism* (translation and commentary by E. Evans, SPCK, 1964). For the early catechumenate, see F. E. Brightman in H. B. Swete, ed., *Essays on the Early History of the Church and the Ministry* (Macmillan, 1918), pp. 320-342; J. A. Jungmann, *The Early Liturgy* (Darton, Longman and Todd, 1960), chap. 7; F. Van der Meer, *Augustine the Bishop* (Sheed and Ward, 1961), chap. 12.

Again, sternly,

> I must warn you in the words of Scripture: Defer it not from
> day to day, for his wrath shall come on a sudden. God knows, I
> myself tremble in my chair when I hear this. I cannot be silent, I
> must make you fearful, being myself full of fear. . . . You say, 'I
> will do it later, tomorrow. Why do you frighten us? Are we not
> promised forgiveness?' Yes, forgiveness is promised, but you have
> no promise of living till tomorrow.

Augustine himself had not been baptized till manhood; he had
prayed, Give me chastity, but not yet.

Sometimes there was panic, an epidemic perhaps or threat of
war, and then people flocked in for instant baptism. When an
earthquake struck Sitifis in Mauretania the inhabitants took to
the fields, and 2000 were baptized. It was the same in the East, in
Jerusalem, Antioch, Constantinople. 'The sacraments are given
us for life, not death,' John Chrysotom tells his people, reminding
them that delay over baptism gives pagans a chance to laugh at
the Church. 'If your philosophy has any force, they say, please
tell us what this multitude of uninitiated means.' And when there
was a crisis, people came in such numbers that the clergy could
not give them even the normal instruction about the sacraments.
He has a story of one such occasion when the bishop was away
and the presbyters feebly baptized all and sundry, even the quite
ignorant. One very young deacon took it upon himself, contrary
to precedent, to carry the catechumens off in groups of a hundred
or so and give them the minimum of sacramental teaching.[3]

Why was this sort of thing going on, and how should bishops
handle it? It must have happened sometimes in earlier days that
men attracted to Christianity were slow to make up their minds or
never could accept all it demanded, somewhat as the God-fearers
in the New Testament adhered to most Jewish religious and
ethical teaching, but would not be circumcised and take the whole
Law upon themselves as a condition of salvation. There might be
something in their work which offended against the strict rules of

[3] J. A. Jungmann, op. cit., pp. 248-49; F. Van der Meer, op. cit.,
pp. 148-51.

Christian discipline, like the participation in idolatrous ceremonies which public officials could hardly avoid or the exercise of capital punishment that fell to magistrates. Such a man might associate with Christians and enroll himself in the inquirer stage of the catechumenate, intending perhaps to be baptized when his public service was over. Constantine himself, baptized only at the end of his life, may be an example of this, and a parallel could be drawn with some African chiefs in modern times. But such men would be few before the age of Constantine, and the fourth century brought an end to the pagan trappings of office which had prevented magistrates from accepting full Christian discipline. In the new situation it was the many, not the few, who delayed their baptism, and not because of idolatrous ceremonies in which they were caught against their wills, but because they hesitated to commit themselves to the full demands of everyday Christian morality—'Give me chastity, but not yet'; something less would do for the time being, they would be Christians of a sort, not pagans. Their hesitation was enhanced by fear of the consequences of sin after baptism. It would be unfair to suggest that these people did not, for the most part, want to live a truly Christian life: they were afraid that they could not live up to its standards. So are we all. Why did their fear take this particular form? Is not Christianity a religion which offers forgiveness to repentance and faith in Christ crucified? Of course that was preached. Yet the conditions of Church life at the time affected the way in which it was preached.

First, on good biblical and evangelistic grounds, the offer of full forgiveness was closely connected with—one might say, concentrated in—baptism. 'Repent and be baptized,' Peter had said, 'every one of you in the name of Jesus Christ for the forgiveness of your sins; and you shall receive the gift of the Holy Spirit. Save yourself from this crooked generation.' Peter's summons at Pentecost was understood as one for immediate action: those who received his word were baptized and there were added that day about three thousand souls—a very primitive mass movement. In different circumstances it could be taken differently, or with a shift of emphasis. When you are ready for baptism, which will mark your final break with this crooked generation, you will receive full pardon for all your sins, you will make a completely new start in the new society, the Church, and you will have the power of the Holy Spirit to live the Christian life. Then, of course, you are assured of salvation if you do live the Christian life. But baptism for the remission of sins can never be repeated. So make sure you really mean it.[4]

Secondly, it had by now been decided that Christian life in the Church should be not only preached as an ideal, but also protected by a practical system of discipline, which will be described in subsequent chapters. Enough for the moment to say that it was severe, that for a time it was held in parts of the Church that there were some sins too grave for any ecclesiastical pardon after baptism (the offender must stay excommunicate), and that for the sins which brought the sinner under this discipline, pardon could only be granted once.

Thirdly, the older practice of a two or three year catechumenate had accustomed people to a relation to the Church less than full membership. They went to church, though not as communicants or office-holders. They counted themselves Christians, they were of the Church, if not in it. We are familiar with similar loose forms of membership today, at home and abroad.

It was therefore tempting to postpone baptism, to keep the opportunity of full pardon in reserve, diminishing the risk of excommunication and damnation through grave post-baptismal sin, yet living in more or less close touch with the Church and behaving on the whole as baptized Christians behaved, perhaps better than some. Again we hear modern voices: 'We don't go to church, but we're just as good Christians as the Smiths next door who go every Sunday. They . . . etc.' Augustine knew the argument: A catechumen sometimes knows more of his religion and leads a better life than many of the baptized. He sees how badly instructed some of them are, and their lives less chaste. . . . Has he the right to draw himself up and say, 'Why should I be bap-

[4] Acts 2.38-41.

tized? Do I need what my inferior in conduct and knowledge
has?' The Lord will answer him, Augustine says, 'How much is
he your inferior? As much as you are Mine?'[5]

Postponement of baptism is understandable; it troubled the
bishops and led to changes in the catechumenate and in discipline.
What emerged was something like this. There was still a preliminary interview with bishop or presbyter, at which sponsors spoke
for the candidate. Then, on the same occasion, a long address was
given by a catechist. We know what it might be like from Augustine's *De catechizandis rudibus*, written for the benefit of a
Carthaginian deacon who was often entrusted with this duty. It
should contain a narration of the story of salvation, mainly from
the Bible but continuing briefly with church history, and a strong
appeal to the will. It should be adapted to the capacity of the
audience. The candidate must profess his willingness to adopt the
Christian way, and then he is given the sacrament of salt and
signed with the cross. He is now a hearer, he goes to church, is
under observation, but apparently does not receive further special
instruction or perform special exercises until he registers for baptism one Easter. This he should do before Lent, during which
concentrated teaching is given in classes and sterner spiritual
exercises are required. At the beginning of Lent the bishop scru-
tinized the candidates, the scrutiny in some places including a
solemn exorcism. They were no longer simple catechumens but
competentes, those who asked for baptism, called in Rome *electi*
and in the East *photizomenoi*, those who are being enlightened.
They must pray much and fast; exorcisms were frequent and
were no mere form, but intended to stimulate the will. Of the
teaching we have an important example in the lectures of Cyril,
Bishop of Jerusalem, to his catechumens, probably in 350. One,
the *Procatechesis*, is a welcome and a general exhortation and
introduction; a set of four lectures next speaks of repentance,
baptism and faith with a doctrinal summary, and then in a set of
twelve the bishop takes them clause by clause through the Creed
of Jerusalem. After baptism on the Saturday evening and first

[5] Aug., *Enarr. in Ps. 90*, II 6.

communion on Easter Day, instruction continues in five addresses, called Mystagogical, which explain more fully the meaning of the eucharist (some scholars attribute these to Cyril's successor, John). Baptism itself had been highly impressive, with immersion in the baptistry, anointing with chrism and the imposition of the bishop's hand for the reception of the Holy Spirit.

Pastorally this organization of Lent and Holy Week was one method by which the Church hoped every year to gather in the reluctant, bring them to the point of decision, instruct them more accurately, and leave them with an unforgettable impression of the crucial step which they had taken.[6]

It was not enough. There is abundant evidence that many were content with enrolment as catechumens and waited a long time before they enrolled as *competentes*. How deeply rooted postponement had become may be seen from the instances so often quoted: of the great Cappadocian Fathers, brought up in deeply Christian families, Basil was baptized at 26, Gregory Nazianzen at 28; Chrysostom was 25; Ambrose had not been baptized when he was chosen Bishop of Milan, nor Nectarius when he was elected Bishop of Constantinople. Augustine became a catechumen when a child, and asked for baptism during a boyhood illness; but his devout mother deferred it when death no longer threatened, and he was 33 at his baptism. A custom apparently so well supported would not be quickly eliminated by episcopal exhortation, even when these very bishops and theologians were saying *mea culpa*. So the catechumenate went on in this form, the gap between preliminary instruction and baptism short or long as the individual decided. It had the merit of flexibility and gave some scope for pastoral advice, but it might leave a local church with a large second-class membership.[7]

---

[6] See J. A. Jungmann, op. cit., pp. 80-84; F. Van der Meer, op. cit., pp. 361-69; E. C. Whitaker, *Documents of the Baptismal Liturgy* (SPCK, 1960). For Cyril's practice and selections from his lectures, W. Telfer in *Library of Christian Classics*, Vol. IV (SCM Press, 1955); and a complete translation in *Nicene and Post-Nicene Fathers*, Vol. VII (Oxford, 1893).

[7] J. A. Jungmann, op. cit., p. 248.

Another answer to the changed situation was the encouragement of infant baptism. This is paradoxical: if adults delay baptism because of the risk to salvation, how will parents be persuaded to have their children baptized? Monica deferred Augustine's baptism, and she was a good Christian woman. But infant baptism was on the increase. It had been allowed from early times. When Tertullian opposed it, that was because it was becoming common. Cyprian strongly advocated it. However, we never have comparative figures, and adult or non-infant baptism may still have been more general in the fourth century. One factor in reversing the trend was the Pelagian controversy of the early fifth century. They taught that infants dying unbaptized were not damned, and while they did not repudiate infant baptism, they reduced it to a kind of blessing and incorporation into the Church. Under the leadership of Augustine, the contrary view prevailed. Baptism is always for the remission of sin; when infants are baptized, it is because they need forgiveness. For what? Original sin, understood as involving guilt and deserving damnation. With the Church's decision against Pelagianism, it was natural for clergy to press infant baptism, as Augustine did, and natural for parents to yield to a pressure which had so much emotional force. In the long run it became the norm, eliminating the catechumenate. Instruction and discipline followed baptism, at which the duties of parents and godparents were inculcated. The dangers are apparent: baptism was dissociated from conversion, while stress upon the efficacy of infant baptism might lead to magical interpretations of this sacrament.

These problems remain, however forcefully the case for infant baptism is stated. In the fifth century the immediate problem of post-baptismal instruction and discipline was eased by the growth of the parochial system. Cathedral baptisms at Easter were now theological and liturgical examples rather than the norm of practice, like cathedral evensong today. If babies are to be baptized, it must be possible near home throughout the year. So parish priests did most of the baptizing, though visiting bishops sometimes baptized, especially in the East. The imposition of hands for the Holy Spirit, however, remained the bishop's prerogative, whether on theological grounds or pastoral, to maintain the unity of the diocese and the direct sacramental ministry of the bishop to all his people. So confirmation, coming some years after baptism, could itself be hedged about with conditions, including instruction and evidence of readiness. As always new practices create their own problems, but given infant baptism, this procedure proved capable of useful development.

For a time the two systems went on side by side: adult baptism, including confirmation, after a fairly serious catechumenate and intense Lenten preparation; and infant baptism, followed by instruction and the Christian home, with confirmation later. But as the latter system was popularized and grounded in teaching on original sin and the danger of dying unbaptized, speedy baptism could hardly be denied to adults who pressed for it; at least, to those in any danger of death. And if instruction can follow baptism, why not make sure that converts are safely incorporated into the Church and so brought under instruction and discipline? Earlier missionaries had not thought like this, but there was something to be said for it, especially when allied with the possibility of mass or tribal conversions. Mark their break with the past by the full solemnities and obligations of baptism. Assure them that they have received remission of all their sins, original and actual, and, washed clean, are making an entirely fresh start at once. Surely they will then respond to moral and intellectual instruction, submitting themselves and their whole culture to Christian influences and building up not individualistic groups but whole Christian communities? An attractive idea; and when the Church was dealing with the Germanic peoples, the catechumenate was drastically reduced, with all emphasis on the subsequent training of a Christian nation. Perhaps that was wrong. Gregory of Tours' picture of 'Christian' Franks is not pleasant; yet a Christian France emerged from it. I am not here pressing this view against the alternative of the gathered congregation, content to wait for a richer and more tested Christianity to make its mark without compromising with the world. I want simply to illustrate what happened and to indicate the problems and choices involved.

The scope of the problems is determined by our answer to the practice of infant baptism. How grave the theological issues are is kept before us by the witness of the Baptists.[8] If, however, on whatever theological grounds, infant baptism is accepted as the norm for all infants indiscriminately, their instruction and pastoral care come after baptism, and this falls within the scope of the next two chapters. If only infants born in Christian families are accepted – a possible position – the preliminary questions put to adults in the early Church will now be put to parents, to ensure the children a chance to grow up in a Christian environment. In some areas acceptance may turn on the marital status of the parents, whether, for instance, they were married by Church rites, or whether the father is monogamous. Since this is in effect a question of whether the parents are themselves maintaining the discipline of the Church, I will defer discussion of it to later chapters. Let us keep now to non-infant baptism and the catechumenate.

Sometimes attitudes to baptism are contrasted as Catholic and Protestant. It is better to look at two distinct positions, and then to recognize that there are possibilities in between them to which both Catholics and Protestants have been drawn from time to time. First, baptism may be connected with conversion and the gathered congregation of the truly converted. Evidence of conversion will be required, and while there may be agreement about the age before which baptism will not be administered (as elsewhere for confirmation), there may be no disciplinary rules laying down a precise period of instruction or moral testing. The emphasis is upon the responsible decision of the candidate, which comes when he is ready, when God elicits it. The minister or congregation will have ways of judging whether this has happened. This is *a* Protestant view, but clearly not *the* Protestant view, since many Protestant churches accept infant baptism, including some which hold the principle of a gathered congregation.

[8] For a review of modern discussion, B. S. Moss ed., *Crisis for Baptism* (SCM Press, 1965).

C

Another view emphasizes incorporation by baptism into the Christian society, the Church, within which the Christian life is built up; it is unnecessary to ask too much at first. This is indeed *a* Catholic view. The Mill Hill Father Thoonen calls it a missiological conversion, adding that if a moral conversion is also demanded, this is an accidental element, a preliminary, the necessity of which depends on circumstances.[9] But we shall see that Catholics have often insisted on a long and exacting catechumenate. In truth, Christians of all kinds have been perplexed about what to demand of a convert as a condition of baptism. The answer turns considerably upon whether one thinks in terms of saving souls, one by one, or of communities, the little community of the family or the bigger one of the clan, tribe or nation.

It has been common missionary strategy to go for the ruler and his close associates. Here are two instances from later history. When the Jesuits reached Mozambique in 1560, Gonzalo da Silveira made for the capital Manica and the ruler, the Monomotapa. 'After a month of training in the catholic faith, the Monomotapa, his favourite wife and sister, and 300 relatives and counsellors, were all baptized.' It was too quick. Soon the ruler was persuaded that Silveira was a sorcerer, ordered him off, and when he refused, had him put to death, together with his latest batch of fifty converts. Meanwhile the Jesuits who stayed nearer the coast had also experienced a reversal. In a few weeks they seemed to have converted all the residents of a chief's village, but their flock fell away when they denounced polygamy and taught that the rain-making ritual was an ungodly superstition.

Mutesa, the Kabaka of Buganda, impressed H. M. Stanley as an intelligent prince who, if aided by virtuous philanthropists, would do more for Central Africa than fifty years of Gospel teaching unaided by such authority. 'In this man I see the possible fruition of Livingstone's hopes, for with his aid the civilization of Equatorial Africa becomes feasible.' Mutesa did not become a

  [9] Thoonen, quoted from J. V. Taylor, *The Growth of the Church in Buganda*, p. 42.

Christian, but welcomed missionaries and helped them with his authority, let some of his pages be instructed (some were to become chiefs, others martyrs), and gave access to what Dr Taylor calls 'the household-clusters of relatives, heads of staff, women, pages and slaves, gathered around the head of the house'. Here was an opening for the transformation of the community, for a Christian Uganda.[10]

Community movements do not necessarily imply speedy mass-baptisms: the problem of a catechumenate remains. We have seen how it was dwindling in the early Church. The historian Socrates, writing about 450, tells of a Burgundian tribe who, pressed by the Huns, thought they would like the help of the strong God of the Romans, decided with one mind to believe in Christ, went in a body to a city in Gaul and asked for baptism. The bishop prepared them, with fasting and instruction, for seven days, baptized them on the eighth, and sent them off to victory. Charlemagne imposed mass-baptism on the defeated Saxons with little if any instruction; but in 796, when conquest of the Avars was imminent, Pippin took episcopal advice on the proper methods, and Paulinus of Aquileia, backed by Arno of Salzburg, protested against hasty baptism. He even pleaded the old rule that, except in emergency, baptism should be administered only at Easter or Pentecost. Catechetical instruction was essential, ignorant clerics should not be allowed to baptize, catechumens must not be enrolled under coercion, but persuaded by preaching. Christ did not say, Go, baptize the nations, and teach them my commandments, but, Go, teach, then baptize. Alcuin wrote to Charlemagne in support of Paulinus' principles.[11]

But how long, how complete an instruction, how severe a moral test? Long enough to mark the gravity of baptism, not too long to discourage eagerness — beyond that a precise answer fitting all circumstances is impossible. We may swing from Bishop Patteson of Melanesia wondering if he has been asking too much, to

[10] J. Duffy, *Portugal in Africa* (Penguin Books, 1962), pp. 89-90; J. V. Taylor, op. cit., p. 28.
[11] Socrates, H.E. VII, 30; Alcuin, *Ep*. 33.

Bishop Neill of South India suggesting that in areas of rapid progress the tendency is to make the conditions of baptism too easy. A theological student once said to him: 'These families have been attending church for three Sundays; shall I arrange for their baptism next Sunday?' Père Lourdel had eight converts baptized within fifteen months of the arrival of the White Fathers in Uganda, not very hasty one would think, yet Cardinal Lavigerie sent an order that all adult enquirers must have four years' training before baptism. Roman Catholic bishops conferring at Dar-es-Salaam in 1912 decided that candidates must spend a year in the Hearers' class and at least two more in the formal catechumenate.[12]

Even more important is the environment in which catechumens live during training. There are not always Christian villages. During the nineteenth century the Jesuits in China established catechumenates, retreat centres to which catechumens were taken, away from pagan associations, for a final preparation lasting some months, after instruction in their own homes and villages by resident catechists for two or more years. I do not know how widely any such plan has been tried or with what success. It may involve a degree of dependence upon the missionary justifiable only so long as it is necessitated.[13]

Length of catechumenate and details of training are matters which have to be decided even with candidates eager for baptism as soon as they are ready and intending to be ready as soon as they can. Quite different is the prolonged catechumenate of those who cannot or will not make up their minds to undertake the full responsibilities of baptism, so that either they themselves are content with this inferior stage of membership or else the catechumenate is being used by the authorities of the Church rather as a restrictive, almost punitive, discipline than a preparatory and

---

[12] C. M. Yonge, *Life of John Coleridge Patteson* (Macmillan, 1874), Vol. I, pp. 343, 367, 383; Vol. II, pp. 303, 372-74, 519-20, 532-33, 540, 546, 551; S. Neill, *The Unfinished Task* (Edinburgh House Press, 1957). pp. 129-30. For Lourdel, J. V. Taylor, op. cit., p. 42.
[13] K. S. Latourette, *History of Christian Missions in China* (SPCK, 1929), pp. 550-51, cf. pp. 331-33.

forward-looking one. In the early Church it was sometimes taught that a youth might delay his baptism until the worst of his sexual temptations was over—over not by conquering them, but by yielding and eventually obtaining remission of his sins. Theologically a parody of Christian principles, this points to practical problems which cannot be brushed aside. At an early date the catechumenate was virtually destroyed and replaced by infant baptism with subsequent instruction and pastoral care. That solution, however, is the very one whose results are now being questioned in the older churches, if not in principle (though this is widely done), then in the practice of baptismal discipline. A second solution is perseverance with the principle of conversion, the élite, however few, the gathered congregation, not worrying about time; one cannot be blind to its strength, provided the elect are not simply regarded as saved from the world, but as its salt and light. Yet it has its drawbacks: it has been a cause of schism, perfectionist groups breaking off in search of an ever more absolute purity of doctrine or morals, or making some one rule the single test of election, and others again breaking away from these groups because they find the demands insupportable.

Further, it is not easy for a gathered and disciplined congregation, even if its members are genuinely humble, to avoid giving the impression that Christianity is only for the few who take it, and not for the likes of me. Nor can we entirely disregard time, sowing and leaving the harvest to God. Expecting a speedy Second Coming, the earliest missionaries erected a severe discipline to protect and prepare those whom they rescued from the world, the flesh and the devil. But as soon as a chance to convert the world appeared, it was discovered that any discipline is fraught with problems. The modern Christian is fighting for his faith under other pressures, secularism, humanism, the renaissance of other great religions, pressures which bear not only upon individuals but whole societies; and, humanly speaking, some of these foes look like winning. Therefore the pastor and evangelist and teacher must think of building up 'the likes of me', long before they are perfect or fully converted, into societies of people who help one another to live by the grace of God. So the thorny problems of discipline, before and after baptism, open up again.

There is no easy solution, but knowledge of the facts helps. In some missionary churches a very high proportion, even 80 per cent, of the adherents are not admitted to communion: either they are delayed catechumens, mostly for disciplinary reasons, or, if baptized, they are under discipline.[14] The existence of a large adult catechumenate, and for such reasons, both unbalances the church and raises questions as to how the individual is to progress. General conclusions will come better when we have considered post-baptismal discipline as well. For the moment let it be repeated that the catechumenate should be kept a preparatory discipline, not a punitive one. Disciplinary details need constant review, and always in the light of the environment, from which it is never easy for the individual to break away. Some religious and moral breaks are absolutely essential, or Christianity would be meaningless. But there are practices which Christianity condemns objectively, but which, in given situations, individuals do not feel to be wrong. Polygamy is an example. There are others, like ancestor-worship or tribal rituals (notably initiation ceremonies) which the Church might be able to transform. To demand absolute repudiation of such institutions as a precondition of baptism is, to say the least, not self-evidently right. Since one cannot expect striking moral progress from the average catechumen living in a bad environment, Christian effort has to be directed upon the whole environment. The disciplinary problems cannot be solved in isolation from the total evangelistic and pastoral problem, and discipline of the individual, pre-baptismal or post-baptismal, must take account of the difficulties he is actually in, the choices open to him, the help he needs. Never should zeal for a system, or even for the holiness of the Church in the abstract, destroy pastoral care for the individual child of God.

[14] Sometimes they fluctuate over short periods between excommunication and good standing — a situation likely to cheapen both discipline and the sacrament which it intends to guard.

CHAPTER FOUR

POST-BAPTISMAL DISCIPLINE:
THE EARLY HISTORY

I

THE SCOTS Confession of 1560 reads:

> The note of the true Kirk of God we believe, confess, and avow to be, first, the true preaching of the Word of God . . . Secondly, the right administration of the Sacraments of Christ Jesus . . . Last, ecclesiastical discipline uprightly ministered, as God's Word prescribed, whereby vice is repressed and virtue nourished.

And there are other Confessions in the Calvinist tradition which make discipline one of the marks of the Church, in distinction for example from the Church of England which, in Article XIX, speaks only of a congregation of faithful men in the which the pure Word of God is preached and the Sacraments be duly ministered. Though, in the *Institutes*, Calvin himself is content, like the Anglicans, with the Word and Sacraments as the formal marks of the Church (*IV. i. 9*), he insists strongly upon the rightfulness and necessity of ecclesiastical jurisdiction and discipline:

> As the saving doctrine of Christ is the soul of the church, so does discipline serve as its sinews, through which the members of the body hold together, each in its own place.

To remove discipline would contribute to the ultimate dissolution of the Church. The purpose of discipline, of which the final stage and sanction is excommunication, is

> First, that they who lead a filthy and infamous life may not be called Christians, to the dishonour of God, as if his holy Church were a conspiracy of wicked and abandoned men; . . . secondly,

that the good be not corrupted by the constant company of the wicked, as commonly happens; . . . thirdly, that those overcome by shame for their baseness begin to repent.

Calvin goes on to explain how the Church exercises this discipline, and while he commends the procedure of the ancient and better Church in some respects, he cannot excuse its excessive severity in others, a severity which led either to great hypocrisy or utter despair (*IV. xii. 1-8*).

What was this procedure of the ancient Church? How did it arise? Was it good, on the whole? And what should the Church do today? There is a prior question: should the Christian Church exercise discipline at all? Is not this Law rather than Gospel and contrary to the freedom with which Christ set us free? It may be argued that the Church should offer to its members all Christ's gifts of Word and Sacrament and other means of grace, should earnestly persuade them towards the Christian life, but never fall back on a legal discipline with sanctions. Such questions must be kept in mind. First, however, let us see what actually happened; for the Church, which is not a disembodied society, did not find it possible to live without rules.[1]

The early Christians had precedents. 'If any man of the house of Israel . . . eats any blood, I will cut him off from among his people.' 'If a person turns to mediums and wizards . . . I will cut him off from among his people. Consecrate yourselves therefore and be holy' (*Lev. 17.10; 20.6, RSV*). Judaism exercised discipline in its synagogues, with excommunication, and there were strict rules in the Qumran community and similar sects. But Jesus, following upon some of the prophets and psalmists, had taught that divine forgiveness is offered freely to repentance, and the Gospel as understood by St Paul reaffirmed the free gift of pardon, grounded in the redeeming acts of Christ and received by repentance and faith. It is this that poses the problem of law and discipline. How is the forgiven community to be kept holy, so as

---

[1] The historical and theological problems are discussed with great learning and insight in K. E. Kirk, *The Vision of God* (Longmans 2nd ed., 1932), to which I am much indebted.

truly to become the body of Christ? Paul saw no contradiction between his gospel of forgiveness and the practice of discipline. The incestuous man at Corinth is to be removed and handed over to Satan. If no integrated system of discipline was presented by the New Testament for obedient acceptance, there were elements from which the young church might construct one:

1. The authority to bind and loose, *Matt. 16, 18*; *John 20*;

2. The requirement that individual offenders submit to the Church on pain of excommunication, *Matt. 18*;

3. Open reproof of sinners (*I Tim. 5.20*) and heretics (*Titus 3.10*);

4. Confession of sins to one another (*James 5.16*);

5. Classification of sins; passages in *Heb. 6, 10, 12* suggest that there is no forgiveness of post-baptismal sin; in *I John 5* there is sin unto death and sin not unto death; in *Mark 3.29* an eternal sin, blasphemy against the Holy Spirit, cannot be forgiven.

6. The decree in *Acts 15.29* makes it a condition of Christian membership to abstain from the pollution of idols, unchastity and blood.

Difficult as these passages are, they lay ready to hand for those who had to take decisions about law and discipline.

II

Before the second century closed a system of ecclesiastical discipline was in force. It was not uniform in detail, and there are obscurities in its early history and in third-century practice. I will first summarize its main features, glossing over difficulties, and then take up the story a little more fully. It was on a diocesan basis, administered by the bishop in person, not by the presbyters individually, though he consulted them. It was public: the fact of sin, but probably not the detail, was confessed in the presence of the congregation. The sinner was publicly reproved and, if suspended from communion, entered the order of penitents, a class recognizable from such outward tokens as sackcloth and ashes.

He had works of satisfaction to perform. When the defined period was over and the works done, he was publicly restored to communion. The system involved a classification of sins. Some, offences which Christians commit from day to day like eating and drinking too much, losing one's temper, gossiping maliciously, were not brought under discipline: these the individual takes straight to God for pardon through repentance. At the other end of the scale were offences so grave that the Church could do nothing but excommunicate the sinner for ever, leaving him to the final mercy of God. In between, the bishop must determine the gravity of the sin and the appropriate penalty. Consequently there was a tendency to draw up codes, so that something like a tariff was established by canon law, progressively limiting the local bishop's discretion. Further, this public discipline for grave sin was available once only. It was *paenitentia secunda*. The first penitence in baptism secured remission of all sin, and baptism could not be repeated. Nor, it was thought, could this second chance; thereafter grave sins must be punished by final excommunication.[2]

So far I have described the system summarily and statically. Like most institutions it was prone to historical change, and like many other institutions of the early Church, we have insufficient evidence about its development. Our information comes piecemeal from different places at various dates, and cannot be pressed into a single pattern. A struggle went on between the champions of severity and the more easy-going or more compassionate. There were differences about the particular sins which should or could be dealt with by this discipline and also about the advisability of having definite rules or codes, about the authority of custom, the extent of episcopal discretion, the legitimacy of making large changes. Passing over purely academic problems, we must consider those of wider significance.

[2] The technical literature is large. B. Poschmann, *Penance and the Anointing of the Sick* (translated and revised by F. Courtney, Burns and Oates, 1964) is a convenient history. Much of the evidence is given *verbatim* in O. D. Watkins, *A History of Penance* (Longmans, 1920), though his discussion is sometimes out of date.

Grave sin was a paradox to the first Christians. How could it be committed by one who is through faith and baptism a new creature, clothed in the righteousness of Christ? 'Whosoever is begotten of God, sinneth not.' The same thought continues after Paul and John. 'The spiritual man cannot do what is fleshly,' says Ignatius. If then a man sins after baptism, is he not really a Christian? Was his baptism unreal? Origen had met people who said, 'If a man believes, he does not sin; if he sins, that proves he does not believe.' Mere theory or plain uncharitableness, perhaps; but there was some inclination to translate the theory into disciplinary action. Although, if II Corinthians 2 refers to the incestuous man of I Corinthians, St Paul had been willing to restore him to fellowship after handing him over to Satan, the Hebrews passages cannot easily be explained away. 'If we sin deliberately after receiving the knowledge of the truth, there no longer remains a sacrifice for sins, but a fearful prospect of judgment.' At least for apostasy, it is impossible to renew again to repentance those who have once been enlightened and become partners of the Holy Spirit, since they are crucifying the Son of God afresh. Hermas (Rome, second century) says he has heard there is no other penitence (*metanoia*) after that one when we went down into the water and received forgiveness. 'You have heard rightly,' the Shepherd tells him, 'so it is.'[3]

This extreme severity was not to win the day. Hermas, fortunately, received a revelation that there was to be *one* chance of forgiveness for grave post-baptismal sin; and this became the controlling principle in ecclesiastical discipline for centuries. But controversy raged round the question: Are any sins so gross that the Church cannot assure the offender of pardon and readmit him, after discipline, into its fellowship, but can only hand him over to the hope of God's mercy? If so, which?

Here the decree of the Council of Jerusalem (*Acts 15*) was important. Its original meaning and application need not detain us: enough that it had to do with Church membership. Later, the

[3] II Cor. 5.17; I John 3.9; 5.18; Ign. *Ephesians* 8; Origen on Romans II, 7; *Hom. in Num.* X, 1; Heb. 10. 26-27; 6.4-6; Hermas, *Mand.* IV, 3.

Eastern Church tended to interpret it as primarily a food or table-fellowship law. In the West it was often taken morally: 'things strangled' was dropped from the text, perhaps correctly, 'things offered to idols' was generalized into idolatry, fornication taken literally and blood explained as bloodshed. So understood, the decree specified the three capital sins totally incompatible with being a Christian, which could easily be given a disciplinary turn: the three sins which must be punished by exclusion from the Church, and perhaps for ever – God himself might never forgive them. In his book *On Chastity*, written about 220, Tertullian explains that the apostles singled idolatry, adultery and murder out from the Decalogue for special attention. 'Not that they allow the others, but these are the only ones which they mention as certainly irremissible.'

When he wrote this Tertullian was already a schismatic, a rigorist Montanist. He is attacking some bishop, either Callistus of Rome or the Bishop of Carthage, for relaxing the Church's discipline concerning adultery. 'The Pontifex Maximus, the bishop of bishops, issues his peremptory edict: I remit the sins of adultery and fornication to those who have performed penance.' There is a historical problem here, and Tertullian may be wrong in claiming that to admit adulterers to penance and thereafter to communion is an innovation. But he must have some ground for his attack, since he confidently uses a *reductio ad absurdum*: the three are tied together in the decree, and if you pardon adultery, you will logically have to pardon apostasy (=idolatry) and murder, which is absurd – you would never do that. Cyprian states categorically that some of his predecessors as Bishop of Carthage 'altogether shut the place of penance (*paenitentia*) against adulteries'. So it must be true that in Africa at one time, and perhaps elsewhere, adulterers were finally excluded from communion, however deeply they repented.

In Cyprian's own day the controversy shifted to apostasy, sacrificing to pagan gods under pressure from magistrates enforcing the edict of Decius (AD 250). There is a strong case for holding that previous disciplinary tradition had opposed the readmission of apostates to communion. Tertullian assumes this, Origen — though inconsistent — sometimes speaks of unforgivable sins, including idolatry, and Cyprian, in a biblical anthology composed before he became a bishop, has a chapter: that he who sins against God cannot have remission in the Church. If there was a widespread rule against reconciliation of penitent apostates, one understands how grave a problem confronted the Church when large numbers lapsed in 250. Were they all lost for ever, or had the Church been too severe in the past? This must be decided by a council. When one met in 251 the decision took the form that hope of reconciliation should not be entirely denied to the lapsed — which sounds like a change—but that, if it was to be granted, the conditions must be stern in order to preserve Gospel discipline. So apparently the Church was compelled by a new situation to give up what had been accepted as an obvious principle well supported by biblical texts.

It is possible, however, that the principle had already been abandoned and that the controversy touched only the precise rules for the reconciliation of apostates. Should this be granted only upon their death-beds, so that they might die in the peace of the Church with assurance of forgiveness, or might it take place earlier, and if so, on what terms? What account should be taken of the exact scope and circumstances of the offence and of the spiritual state of the offender? But even if the range of dispute is thus limited, it remains true that there was a clash between more and less severe views of what should be done. Cyprian himself moved from a stern, though not completely rigorist, position to a gentler one, the decisions of his council of 252 were milder than in 251 (see how the rot sets in, rigorists could say), and in Rome the new bishop Cornelius was regarded by many as altogether too easy-going.[4]

As for the third capital sin, the earliest evidence of reconciliation of a wilful homicide is a canon of the Council of Ancyra in

[4] For Cyprian's problems see his *De Lapsis* and many of his letters; B. Poschmann, op. cit., pp. 52-62, with references to other discussions; O. D. Watkins, op. cit., I, ch. 4.

314: he may be enrolled as a penitent, but can be admitted to communion only on his death-bed.

So absolute and final excommunication of penitents drew to its end, though lingering here and there. Soon after the persecution of Diocletian, about 306, a Spanish council met at Elvira, and several of its canons finish inexorably, 'it is decreed that he cannot be reconciled even at the end'. But the ecumenical Council of Nicaea, 325, decided that all penitents should be reconciled at the moment of death.[5]

As time goes on, the severer side of discipline shows itself not in the ultimate refusal of pardon, but in the exclusion of sinners from full reconciliation and communion for very long periods or for life, and in the attempt to keep the rule of one public penance and pardon only. The penitent was not wholly cut off from the life of the Church. He was rather like a catechumen, attending part of the eucharist, doing spiritual exercises, advancing by stages towards reconciliation. But his spiritual progress could not be assisted by full participation in the sacramental life of the Church, nor could he hold office. It was still a very severe system, and we shall see how it broke down.

III

Confronting this severity there was always a milder trend whose exponents might base themselves upon scriptural teaching on forgiveness or upon pastoral necessity as they saw it. According to his opponent Hippolytus, Callistus of Rome relaxed the discipline in several ways. 'He was the first to make concessions to men's pleasures, saying that all sins are remitted by him'; and if this is a biased account, there is also Tertullian's attack on Callistus or another leading bishop for taking a laxer view of adultery as not beyond ecclesiastical pardon. During the Decian persecution, a strong party in Africa wanted to restore the lapsed on easier terms than Cyprian's. The Church moved on towards the

[5] O. D. Watkins, ch. 6, for these councils.

new conditions of the fourth century with an essentially severe discipline, but with a considerable pull towards relaxing it.

Sometimes opposition to relaxation erupted into schism. Montanists believed that the Church was yielding to the world, and as a remedy stood for extreme severity in mode of life and punishment of sin. Idolatry, adultery and bloodshed after baptism were certainly irremissible – and their connotation was stretched. To the unforgivable sins Tertullian once adds fraud and bad faith. The milder treatment of the lapsed in 251 was countered by the Novatianists who took up the position that apostasy can never be pardoned and broke away to form a separatist church of the pure. After the Diocletianic persecution, the Donatists broke off from the Church in Africa on the ground that it had compromised itself by communion with apostates and thereby lost its holiness and ceased to be the true Church. These schisms point to the development of rival doctrines of the Church springing from conflicting ideas of the holiness of the Church and the communion of saints. As the perfectionists saw it, the Church can be corrupted to the point of destruction by the impurity of its members; and they picked on particular relaxations of discipline as proof that this had happened. Callistus, on the other hand, taught that wheat and tares must be allowed to grow together in the Church until the harvest, like Noah's Ark in which dogs and wolves and crows and all clean and unclean animals lived together on the way to salvation. Cyprian took the same line, which became normal; Augustine used the argument against the Donatists. The holiness of the Church had to be understood more objectively as consisting in the possession or indwelling of the Holy Spirit and in the holy things, Word and Sacrament, which the Church brought to its members. It is a school for sinners, not an exclusive society of perfect saints.[6]

Still, the morality of the members does matter, and most felt that discipline should remain strict. The rule of one public penance only was preserved and so were many of the features

[6] See my *Schism in the Early Church*, 2nd ed. (SCM Press, 1964), ch. 6.

which sharpened discipline by making it public. Further, if the gravest sins were pardonable after all, suitable penances and adequate periods of excommunication must be prescribed for them. In some quarters these were so long that the offender had little hope of reconciliation until he was dying; and there were some who argued, despite the Nicene ruling that all should then be pardoned, that communion should only be granted if the dying sinner had already given satisfactory evidence of true penitence by his works. Throughout the fourth century, at least in the Eastern Church, the classification of sins and tariffing of penances continued, in order to deal more consistently with the new masses of ordinary sinful Christians.

The problems raised by codification are well illustrated by the three *Canonical Letters* which Basil of Caesarea sent to his friend Amphilochius of Iconium in 374-75. To a considerable extent he feels bound by existing canons and customs, and so he approves sentences of excommunication running up to twenty or thirty years, allowing case-law to introduce some clemency by multiplying distinctions and grading offences more minutely than in earlier practice. But codification clearly worries him. It will often be better to have no fixed rule. When sinners improve during penance, the minister entrusted by God with authority to bind and loose can show mercy and shorten the allotted period. Since all disciplinary rules are intended to test the fruits of repentance, 'we judge not by time, but by the manner of the penitence'. Yet, he insists, the Church must maintain its witness against sin, and if sinners do not adequately repent, we must be separated from them and save our own souls from eternal damnation.[7]

What then are the ultimate principles behind public penitential discipline? Witness to the world and the purity of the Church appear to demand a canon law with known penalties; the pastoral care of the individual pulls the other way. Perhaps some of the lengthy sentences were *ad terrorem*, rarely enforced. Before we take these issues further, let us glance at the West.

[7] O. D. Watkins, op. cit., I, pp. 261-64, 267-68, 294-97; Basil, *Letters* 188, 199, 217.

Here there is little evidence of tariffing offences and penalties, and even when canon law defines offences, much is left to the bishop. Thus, quite explicitly, at the Council of Carthage, 397: 'The lengths of penances are to be decided by the bishop's judgment according to the differing qualities of the sins.' While this may indicate a legalist outlook emphasizing the power of the bishop as judge, it may equally be intended to safeguard his discretion as pastor. One gets the impression that the periods of excommunication were comparatively short in the West, with some exceptions, as when Pope Siricius would reconcile apostates only on their death-beds. Severity is shown in a different manner, not heard of in the East, namely the imposition of restrictions upon the penitent for the rest of his life even after readmission to communion. When, for instance, in the first known papal decretal (AD 385), Siricius directs that those who have done penance and then return like dogs to their vomit must return to the state of penitent for the rest of their lives, since they cannot do penance again, he does not mean that they have committed their old sins again, but that they are disregarding the disabilities imposed upon them when they were reconciled. They must not become soldiers, must not marry, or if married must not have intercourse, and, generally, must not indulge in pleasant amusements. In other words, after public penance, for which the period might be fairly short, the restored Christian could not resume ordinary life in the world, in the occupations and with the pleasures allowed to others, but must live an ascetic, quasi-monastic life. Another measure of severity extended the meaning of excommunication in the worst cases from exclusion from the eucharist to a more complete, though perhaps temporary, banishment from life in the Church.[8]

The Eastern Church's long penances and the Western Church's post-penitential disabilities failed to maintain a high and comprehensive standard of discipline, for people simply would not submit themselves to it. As, formerly, some had postponed baptism in order to procure free and complete remission towards the end

[8] Siricius, *Ep.* 1, O. D. Watkins I, p. 369; K. E. Kirk, op. cit., p. 228.

of their lives, so now many deferred their one act of penance
either to a late stage of life or until the approach of death, when
it was accepted that all can be reconciled, and without the accom-
paniment of penances, disabilities and publicity.

This reluctance set the bishops a problem: either they could
exhort people not to postpone penance or they could soften its
rigours. There was no immediate and uniform answer, but trends
of thought can be observed. First, as already to some extent in
Basil, there was a move to limit the offences treated by ecclesiastical discipline to the few considered most grave. There had
always been sins for which no one was expected to undergo
formal discipline, and gradually this class was extended. The
Spanish Council of Toledo (400) defined the term 'ex-penitent'
as: one who after baptism has done public penance for homicide
or certain crimes and very grave sins, and been reconciled. In
Africa, a trifle later, St Augustine knows some who think that
only the three deadly sins, unchastity, idolatry, murder, should be
punished by excommunication, while all others can be expunged
by almsgiving. And though he rejects this as a disciplinary principle, it comes natural to him to specify these three when preaching on penance:

Who are the penitents properly speaking? Those excommunicated for a grave sin: perhaps adultery, perhaps murder, perhaps
some sacrilege, a grievous wound, deadly – but the physician is
all-powerful.

This trend means that a wide range of sin – for many Christians
all their sins – becomes a matter only for pastoral direction,
forgiveness being between God and the conscience, obtained by
repentance and prayer and, as generally believed, by good works.[9]

Secondly, the penalties might be reduced. Basil shows this in
the case of fornication. Pope Innocent was once asked how to
treat those who lived thoroughly unchaste lives after baptism
and asked for penance and reconciliation only at the end of their

---

[9] Toledo, O. D. Watkins I, p. 399; Aug. *Sermon* 352, O. D. Watkins
I, p. 385.

lives. We are milder these days, he said. He takes the lapsed as an example: once they were never readmitted to communion, later they were admitted on their death-beds (cf. pp. 77-78). Circumstances change discipline. Or the post-baptismal disabilities might be eased. For instance, Pope Leo distinguishes between what is owed and what may be voluntarily surrendered from love of perfection, between what is required and what is advised as better. Penitents do well not to engage in commerce, but honest business is not forbidden. He will not allow them to join the army, but if a young man has become a penitent through urgent fear of death or peril of captivity (observe that young men do not usually do penance) and wants later to marry rather than indulge in fornication, this, though not correct, is a venial matter. I am not making a rule, Leo says, but assessing what is tolerable. Leo's concessions are not great, but once there are any, there can be more.[10]

Third, unpleasant publicity might be reduced. Certainly it was excused when it would bring danger to the sinner from State action. We know this from Basil and Augustine, though it may have been an older concession. Leo condemned an attempt to make sinners write down the details of their sins, which would be read out publicly; this is an unhealthy innovation. Next, clergy might more or less acquiesce in the postponement of public ecclesiastical penitence. A council of Orleans (538) reveals contemporary ideas of penitence, which it calls conversion, the adoption of a new (and better?) state of life. No one is to presume to give the *blessing* of penitence to young persons; nor to married people unless both parties agree, and then only at a ripe age. About the same time Caesarius of Arles, who in many sermons warned his folk not to risk deferring penance until their death-beds, acknowledges the difficulties caused by penitential disabilities. He puts the case against his own exhortations. Suppose someone replies, 'I am a soldier, I have a wife. How *can* I do penance?' Caesarius is driven to distinguish between the outward and inner states. 'A penitential life can be lived without coming

[10] Innocent, *Ep.* 6. O. D. Watkins I, p. 370; Leo, *Ep.* 167, O. D. Watkins I, pp. 374-75.

forward to the one public penance.' But is this not effectively the end of any general system of discipline? It becomes something for the few, either because they are criminals and the Church is acting for the State, or because some grave sinners turn specially pious, or because the minority of outstandingly pious Christians voluntarily enter the order of penitents as a form of asceticism. The 'penitent' has become a hero, like the monk.[11]

A viable system of discipline for rank-and-file Christians must involve radical changes. One such change came, at last, in a challenge to the long-accepted principle that penance, as so far understood, could not be repeated. The Western Church clung tenaciously to this rule through the fourth and fifth centuries and much of the sixth, yet its biblical and theological foundations were shaky. In the East one influential voice was raised in favour of a revolution. Both as a presbyter at Antioch and as Bishop of Constantinople, John Chrysostom showed himself a liberal in penitential matters. He did not use a tariff of penalties, insisting rather on the minister's discretion and upon conduct, not time. Five days' real penitence with fasting and prayer is enough to cover a multitude of sins – even one day. And Christians should take their sins directly to God. 'I don't force you to come into the theatre in public, God says. Tell your sins privately to me alone.' So far, this would find some support elsewhere. Chrysostom is not attacking or by-passing the public discipline in suitable cases and pastorally managed. But apparently he took a further step. When he was on trial before his enemies at the Synod of the Oak (403), he was charged among other things with offering immunity to sinners by saying, 'If you sin again, repent again; and whenever you sin, come to me and I will heal you'. According to the historian Socrates, while canon law offered only one occasion of penance after baptism, Chrysostom dared to say, Repent and come a thousand times. For which many of his acquaintances condemned him.

[11] Detailed references for this paragraph are given in K. E. Kirk, op. cit., pp. 504-08.

Though Chrysostom was condemned then, some time in the sixth century the public discipline disappeared from the Byzantine church. The same trend of thought was gathering force in the West. Most of the direct evidence for this century shows rather the decay of the old system than the rise of the new, and the Council of Toledo in 589 is usually quoted as the last attempt to uphold the rule of one penance only. It is execrable presumption to demand reconciliation every time one has sinned. The old order must be enforced, with one penance only. Those who fall back into sin during penance or after reconciliation must be condemned with the severity of the ancient canons. This council, called soon after King Reccared's conversion to mark the reconciliation of the Arian Goths to the Catholic Church, intended to determine the character of the future Spanish church; but in this respect it was fighting against the tide.[12]

What happened? Logically the abandonment of the rule, one penance only, could have led to a reformation of public penance under the bishop in a milder form, practicable and perhaps meeting the necessities of individual pastoral care. It did not work out that way. Publicity was disliked, and it was known that a private system already prevailed in monasteries. Moreover, many were by now used to an informal private discipline, based on spiritual counselling, which put the emphasis more on the assurance of forgiveness, absolution, than on public witness to the Church's standards of holiness. Add the quickening development of the parochial system, which meant that most people knew their priest and few their bishop, and it is easy to see how, about this time, a complete revolution was effected, so that public discipline was replaced, except as sheer punishment, by the private confession and absolution administered by the parish priest, with penances following instead of preceding absolution. In western Europe this revolution was consolidated by the Celtic missionaries to the Continent who took with them from these islands a system of private, though still tariffed, discipline allowing for repetition, a

---

[12] Chrysostom, O. D. Watkins I, pp. 300-17; K. E. Kirk, pp. 280-83; Toledo, O. D. Watkins II, p. 567.

system which had grown up among them while they were more or less isolated from continental developments.[13]

So much for a sketch of the history. The next chapter will consider the theological and pastoral lessons or problems to which this story may give rise, and will draw some parallels with the life of the churches today.

[13] For the Celtic system, O. D. Watkins II, pp. 587-631; K. E. Kirk, pp. 279-91; B. Poschmann, op. cit., pp. 122-35. For the texts, L. Bieler, *The Irish Penitentials*, a critical edition with introduction and English version, Dublin, 1963. Generally for the transition to private penance, R. C. Mortimer, *The Origins of Private Penance*, Oxford, 1939.

CHAPTER FIVE

POST-BAPTISMAL DISCIPLINE:
PRINCIPLES AND PROBLEMS

I

THE LAST chapter described the rise and fall of a system of public discipline and its replacement by 'going to confession': private confession to the parish priest, absolution, personal direction, with private penances following. Not that the older practice disappeared entirely. An effort to reintroduce it was made in Charlemagne's time, and throughout the Middle Ages it was used for special cases. It won new prominence and vigour at Geneva under Calvin, then in Scotland and New England. In old England the Puritans favoured it, while the Church of England retained ecclesiastical courts, punishing fornication and threatening excommunication to make people pay their tithe or church-rates. Still, the coming of the private system was a revolution. Until the Reformation and for most of Christendom afterwards, this was how the sins of ordinary Christians were disciplined. We must analyse more systematically the causes of this change.

It was not due only to low average standards, the sort of thing Caesarius of Arles reveals when he says that fornication is so rife among young men and so little blamed that he, as bishop, cannot excommunicate them all. Nor only to the people's feeling that penalties were too severe, or their desire for complete remission of sins at the close of their lives. Not even to all these put together. It was also because many bishops felt that some of its features were pastorally unsatisfactory, and not primarily because it was so severe, though some thought this, but because it was in danger of being legalistic or mechanical. The good pastor saw that the remedy lay neither in increasing the rigorism nor in reducing canonical penalties, but in examining the individual's spiritual condition and the circumstances of his offence. Graded tariffing indeed helped. Instead of ruling that every act of idolatry or apostasy entailed life-long excommunication, it was asked exactly what had been done and under what compulsion, after what struggle with one's own weaknesses. Cyprian had made broad distinctions of this kind, which the Council of Ancyra (314) curiously elaborated: for those attending an idol-feast under compulsion, three years' excommunication if they wore dark clothes and wept, but if they went with cheerful faces and fine clothes, six years! This canon adds: 'the bishop has authority to test conduct and either to be merciful or to increase the time; above all, let the life be examined and mercy be measured out accordingly.'[1] This was the true way of advance, rather than its case-law, since grading penalties is only a compromise. Still, episcopal or congregational discretion cannot dispense with principle (the emotion of pity can be capricious), and the Church was impelled to reflect more deeply upon the aims of discipline, with results which I must now summarize in general terms, with occasional comment.

First, discipline maintains the holiness of the Church corporately, so that it may make a pure offering of itself to God. The Bride of Christ must be pure. Strong feelings of this kind were behind the rigorist or perfectionist schisms which made the actual moral holiness of the members a test of the reality of the Church, of its *esse*, as we say nowadays. The bishops must nurse the aspirations after holiness, without the rigorist conclusion. They could do three things. They could turn the false inference by working out a positive doctrine of the holiness of the Church, in which the Holy Spirit dwells and through which Christ offers his holy things – Word, sacrament, fellowship – to the forgiven but not yet fully sanctified members. They could explore the mercy of God, which is not inconsistent with his own holiness, the love which first loved us and gave his Son who, while we were yet sinners, died for us (not that rigorists denied this, but their thinking

[1] Ancyra, canons 4, 5, 6.

might not be true to it); and they could keep asking what sort of discipline is consistent with the God revealed and active in Christ.

Besides this Godward movement, there was the need to demonstrate the holiness of the Church to men. In the missionary situation of the early Church, it was obviously part of its evangelistic duty both to disperse the slanders which were spread abroad about Christians — as so often in later times — and to demonstrate its moral superiority to other religions, in the hope that this would attract converts. This was all the more necessary in that it was offering forgiveness to sinners and unashamedly taking in the wicked who repented and the foolish and illiterate lower classes — a gang of discredited and proscribed desperadoes, one opponent called them, the lowest dregs of the populace, a secret tribe that lurks in darkness, shunning the light.[2] This is why some argued that the public discipline should deal primarily, or even exclusively, with public sins, those which bring open scandal upon the Church, and not with private ones; a dangerous distinction morally, but understandable in so far as the purpose of discipline is to protect the good name of the Church in the eyes of society. This purpose, however, may seem less urgent in proportion as Christianity becomes the generally accepted religion in a particular society, as for instance in mediaeval Europe. Then the emphasis may shift from the prestige or quality of the Church corporately to the effect upon the individual penitent.

Secondly, there was a special desire to protect the sanctity of the eucharist. 'Cast not your pearls before swine,' was quoted. St Paul had closely related his exhortations against unchastity and idolatry to the eucharist. He who joins himself to a prostitute becomes one body with her. Your bodies are members of Christ. Shall I take the members of Christ and make them members of a prostitute? The cup and the bread are a participation in the blood and body of Christ. You cannot drink the cup of the Lord and the cup of demons. Whoever eats the bread or drinks the cup of the Lord unworthily will be guilty of profaning the body and blood of the Lord. Let a man examine himself, and so eat of the bread

[2] Minucius Felix, *Octavius* 8.

and drink of the cup. Else, he will be bringing judgment upon himself.[3] Fear of such profanation is a worthy sentiment, and fear of punishment, if less worthy, must have been effective in practice. So it was felt, on grounds not wholly applicable to baptism, that this sacrament must be guarded, the table must be fenced. This conviction does not lead inevitably to a penitential system of the kind built up in the early Church, in which the penitent is made to wait years for restoration to communion. It may be, as some Fathers were coming to think, that where repentance is sincere and there is a will to reform, reconciliation should be granted at once in order to strengthen the will through the sacramental life. Perhaps this is the proper conclusion in so far as discipline aims at the recovery of individuals, and perhaps only the impenitent and the 'open and notorious evil liver' should be excluded. But in practice discipline had usually been directed not only upon the spiritual good of the individual, but also upon vindicating the good name and moral standards of the Church collectively, the Church which is made most manifest in the eucharistic act and must there be manifestly pure. This is probably a bad argument, since none are pure or worthy except through repentance and forgiveness; but the feeling behind it has been very powerful.[4]

There is a further complication: sins committed one by one can be repented one by one, even if they are repeated. But there are continuing states which may be thought wrong in themselves and are of such a nature that they cannot be said to have been repented of unless they are abandoned. A familiar instance is remarriage after divorce. If it is wrong in itself, or if one's own church forbids it, what exactly does repenting it mean? Confessing that the second marriage is adultery, and separating? Returning to the first partner? The disciplinary problems are obvious. They are quite similar when Christianity is taken into a polygamous society. The Church feels it should demonstrate its moral

[3] I Cor. 6.15-17; 10.16-21; 11.27-29.
[4] Protection of the Holy Communion was a very prominent motive in Calvin.

principles and maintain its corporate rules, though at the same time it knows it must care for the individual who, to the Church, is never expendable, as useless soldiers might be dismissed from an efficient army. Even so, it is not axiomatic that exclusion from the eucharist is the right way to protect standards. Participation may be the way of healing; it may be that Christ will suffer the affront as he suffered the Cross, to redeem. He cannot be corrupted. Perhaps the Holy Communion is most honoured when there is confidence in the sanctifying power of its holiness.

Sometimes, in the early Church, instead of excommunicating offenders, the clergy warned them to stay away from the eucharist, imposing upon themselves a private and informal penance until they believed themselves fit to return. Caesarius of Arles gives such advice. Since this was milder than canonical penance and also evaded the rule of one penance only, such well-intentioned pastoral care may have been useful. But its danger is to be seen in churches today – especially among Protestants? – when people go to evensong but 'don't feel good enough to go to communion', or regard those who do go as a specially pious inner group rather than as the normal members of the Church.

Next it must be pointed out that in so far as discipline is based on fear of actual moral contamination by evil-doers, this is not averted by exclusion of the offender from the eucharist alone, so long as he is allowed to come to church and take part in Christian social life. If he is a corrupting influence, he will corrupt there. That is in part why some perfectionist sects have wanted total exclusion of sinners and have tried to be societies of holy saints, however small. The early Church encouraged the penitent to attend the first part of the eucharist, like the catechumen, and generally to remain in a positive relation to the Church, which risked contamination to that extent, as was surely right.

II

We are asking on what principles a bishop of the early Church might exercise his discretion; and so far we have had him thinking in terms of guarding the holiness of the Church as a Godward offering, as a demonstration to the world, and as protecting the members from corruption by evil companions. When he turns to consider the sinner individually, what are the aims of discipline? To punish, to deter, to cure? or some combination of these? Most people believed in retributive justice. Sin (or in the State, crime) *ought* to be punished, a principle which tends to carry with it the corollary: and punished appropriately. But unlike purely moral theorists, a Christian bishop could not leave God out. 'Vengeance is mine, saith the Lord: I will repay.'[5] It is God himself who vindicates his moral order and inflicts retribution, above all the final penalty, damnation. That was one accepted principle. The second was that God is loving and merciful, and forgives. How these things can both be true is the problem which underlies the doctrine of the Atonement, which in turn underlies Christian discipline. Perhaps some bishops did think of themselves as God's agents in administering retributive punishment, just as the secular ruler is his agent in punishing crime simply because it ought to be punished. On the whole, however, they were thinking about the effects of punishment and left retribution, strictly speaking, to God. If a man was totally and finally excommunicated, it was in order to save the Church from contamination and to drive the sinner to seek divine forgiveness. Other penalties also, even life-long excommunication, had the consequences in view: they were deterrent to others and remedial, it was hoped, to the offender. With certain differences of emphasis, the pastoral purpose was frequently affirmed.

Sentences of three, five, fifteen years' excommunication look like retributive punishment, inflicted because the offence deserves that particular penalty, and they may often have been pronounced in that spirit. Yet in principle graded penalties are compatible with deterrent or remedial punishment. The subtler and graver danger of such a system lies elsewhere. Codifying sins and tariffing sentences leads easily to an external idea of sin. The sin is defined, pin-pointed. Has it been committed? Yes. All right, so

---

[5] Rom. 12.19.

much punishment. It was never as crude as that, which would be altogether legalistic, for the Church required repentance as well as penances as the condition of reconciliation. It tried to deal with sin, St Paul's *hamartia*, as well as with sins, *hamartemata*. And, as we have seen, it constructed a kind of case-law which took account of variations within a class of sins, and of the sinner's moral condition and any mitigating circumstances. There was a dilemma: more and more nice tariffing and more and more episcopal discretion. Increase the tariffing, and you probably become more legalistic. Increase the discretion, and you may get chaos or a feeling that justice is not being done. There is stimulus to thought in the secular parallel, where the offence is defined by known law, the fact decided by a jury, the sentence determined by a judge who has discretion, but only within such limits as shall not appear to travesty a commonly accepted sense of justice or reduce a society founded upon law to disorder.

But that is only an analogy, for again the Christian has to bring God in. Not only is retribution in God's hands; so, in the end, is forgiveness, free and undeserved, not earned or merited. In moral thinking punishment has reward as its correlative. Reward is a difficult notion to Christians, who cannot shut their eyes to Jesus' frequent use of it, yet must say 'We are all unprofitable servants', and know that whatever good they do is done by the grace of God; it is not their own unaided work, which they can honestly put in for a prize. Reward was dangerously prominent in early Christian ethics. While still a catholic, Tertullian was very blunt: 'God is just, so a good deed puts God in your debt.'[6] The next step in this theory of merit is to apply it even to penitential works. They are satisfactions, compensations, which square the account, discharge your debt, put you right with God. How can he in justice withhold the forgiveness which you have earned? The conclusion was tempting, and theologians and ordinary folk alike came to believe that much sin could be purged by almsgiving and other good works. At worst, others could do the works and the sinner pay for them. Rather better, repentance was taken to be

* Tertullian, *On Repentance*, 2; K. E. Kirk, op. cit., pp. 130-46.

implicit in the performance of the works. But it was only too easy to forget that, while good works, including compensation to the injured and satisfaction to God, may be excellent in themselves, repentance is the condition of forgiveness and reconciliation with God.

Holding firmly to this truth as his guiding principle, a pastorally minded bishop who was already using his discretionary powers to adapt discipline to individual cases might go a step further and question the traditional system as a whole. It seems a fair conclusion that its transformation into something very different resulted not only from popular dislike and refusal to submit to it, but also from theological and pastoral concern among the clergy.

The new system had the advantage of general acceptance — a great advantage, since discipline is a practical matter which fails if it cannot be put into practice. It became the basis of ordinary church life, with the older public discipline of excommunication kept in reserve. In itself it has considerable merits, at any rate in a settled Church and society, a Christendom. This system is familiar in its western form: infant baptism, instruction, confirmation, admission to communion, pastoral care of adults in a responsible full membership; then, to deal with sins, opportunity to the clergy for private admonition in a pastoral unit not too large for personal knowledge, confession, absolution upon repentance, followed by spiritual exercises or works not intended to earn forgiveness but to promote moral and spiritual growth and, where necessary, to compensate an injured fellow-man, not God. At its best this is a thoroughly pastoral and personal ordering of Christian life. Are the defects which have shown themselves in the course of history defects of principle, intrinsic to the system, or have they been due to abuse of what is good in itself by human folly and sin?

What are the defects? First, it never quite shook free from tariffing, the legalistic element in the older discipline. This is notable in the early Middle Ages. The very Celtic books which helped to establish private and repeatable confession and absolution present a complicated system of tariffs. Secondly (and this also is true of the Celtic and Frankish books) penances could be commuted for cash or performed by a substitute. Though theoretical defences of some sort can be suggested for such concessions, they really put the system back on a mechanical basis. Third, the ordinariness of the confessional, the privacy, the repetition, the almost routine connexion with going to communion next day, has often been thought to produce a light attitude to sin and to weaken the call for genuine repentance. This criticism is applied also to modern times:

As modern penances are so slight [says a recent manual of Catholic teaching] it is desirable that penitents should increase their value by earnestness in their accomplishment, by other works, and by gaining indulgences.

Fourth, the system is attacked for its clericalism, as a result of which — it is argued — growth in moral personality is hampered, since the layman does not take enough decisions for himself and is kept too long in the position of an obedient child. Legalism and clericalism are even more apparent — the argument runs — where it is taught that forgiveness *cannot* be obtained for grave sin without recourse to the clergy and where sacramental absolution is made a condition of participation in the Holy Communion.

It may not be easy to decide which of these defects are intrinsic to the system or highly probable effects of it, and which are abuses of it. *Abusus non tollit usum* is an excellent theoretical maxim. In practice a system may be repudiated because of abuse, as happened at the Reformation. And having broken with the existing system, the Protestant churches had next to define their own principles. In a word, Protestants have held that the layman is not bound to confess even grave sin to the minister as a condition of forgiveness, nor, unless he has been formally put under discipline, as a condition of eucharistic fellowship. But, to prevent this theological principle from working out too individualistically, some Protestant churches have revived, even in severe forms, something like the public discipline of the early Church without the rule against repetition. Just in so far as this discipline is *not*

intended to secure forgiveness (which comes through repentance
and faith) but rather to preserve the purity of the Church, it may
run into legalism again and may be punitive in its operation. In
many Protestant churches discipline in this formal sense is practically unknown.

III

All the problems of discipline press hard upon a missionary
church in a non-Christian environment. Our situation at home is
making us face questions of this kind with a new seriousness, but
while we are mostly at the stage of discussion only, churches and
missions overseas have long been compelled to act, and therefore
to choose. They might work out their discipline afresh from the
Bible and their own Christian sense in their own circumstances.
Or they could look to the past for guidance, and then might either
hold to the practice of their mother-churches, modifying details
rather than principles, or come under the influence of churches
working near them, churches whose ways were unfamiliar to their
sponsors at home. All very confusing, especially to converts aware
of the controversies and rivalries of the churches which had come
to them.

Does the early Church help? Not by providing a ready-made
pattern of discipline, but by provoking the search for principles
and for the causes of historical change. Let us look at some
concrete cases.

Prominent among the disciplinary problems which run through
Church history are those touching traditional festivals and ceremonies. The early Church went a long way with 'baptizing' pagan
festivals. Bede connects the word Easter with the Anglo-Saxon
spring-goddess Eostre, and the Resurrection theme was apt to take
into itself the rejoicings over a new Spring. Christmas has a
Christian name, but its date was chosen to counter the birthday of
Sol Invictus, and perhaps also to substitute an innocent cheerful-
ness for the licence of the Saturnalia. So far, so good. It is less easy
to assess the consequences of replacing the cults of local gods or
holy places by the veneration of local saints. One may perpetuate

the old instead of establishing the new; polytheism creeps back. To quote Latourette:

At Siena the Temple of Quirinus became the Church of S. Quirino and thus a pagan god was given Christian canonization. The transfer of Aphrodite Pelagia into St Pelagia seems to be proved.

The multitudinous local cults of the Madonna have aroused strong suspicions and powerful antagonisms, however careful the official teaching.[7]

In his *Confessions* (*VI, 2*), Augustine tells how his mother, while staying at Milan, took bread and wine to the tomb-chapels of the saints, as she did at home in Africa. But the sacristan stopped her: Ambrose had forbidden any offerings. Monica had never taken more than a sip of wine at each tomb, but she obeyed the bishop who thought these funeral feasts were occasions of drunkenness and too much like the pagan superstition of the *Parentalia*, the Roman cult of ancestors. When he became a presbyter at Hippo, Augustine wrote to the Primate of Carthage pleading with him to suppress the cult-meals at martyr-tombs, which suggested official toleration of drunkenness. 'For who dare forbid in private what is done in holy places and called a tribute to the martyrs?' Besides, he says, these drunken revels in cemeteries are commonly thought by the carnal and ignorant laity to comfort the dead, as well as honour the martyrs. Without denying that the spirits of the dead may be benefited, he thinks the offerings had better be given to the poor in coin. We may conclude that, at its best, the early Church was watchful against abuses. But some objected to any adaptations, pressing for a clean break. They may have been right.

The most striking controversy over ceremonies took place in China in the seventeenth and eighteenth centuries. Dressed as Confucian scholars, the Jesuits tried hard to win the confidence of the ruling and educated classes and to understand and respect Chinese customs. Though many could not be tolerated by Chris-

[7] K. S. Latourette, *Expansion* I, p. 321; cf. J. A. Jungmann, op. cit., pp. 133-51, 182-87.

D

tians, others might be innocuous, or easily made so. Among the latter were the ceremonies in honour of ancestors and of Confucius. It would scarcely be possible to eradicate them, since opposition to their use by Christians would slow up evangelization and perhaps even lead the State to prohibit missionary work. Matteo Ricci decided that the rites were purely civil and that Christians could take part in them. The Christian conscience should have time for reflection. Christian forms of burial and honouring the dead would, he hoped, prevail in the end. A long controversy ensued, with conflicting instructions from Rome following one upon another. At one point the Jesuits obtained a declaration from the friendly emperor K'ang Hsi that Confucius was honoured simply as a legislator and that the ancestor-rites did not ask them for protection, but demonstrated affection and commemorated their good deeds. Further opposition from Rome so provoked him that he came near expelling the mission, but compromises (the Eight Permissions) prolonged the uncertainty until in 1742 Rome forbade Christians to use these ceremonies. It remains an open question whether a larger and stronger Christian church could have been established in China during the seventeenth century if sympathetic backing had been given to the Jesuit policy of assimilation and adaptation, or whether the rejection of such compromises was necessary to prevent a syncretism which would have blunted the Church's cutting-edge. The matter was not decided entirely on its merits, such was the rivalry between Jesuits and Dominicans at the time. The modern parallel of playing off denominational variations in discipline against each other will not escape notice.[8]

The problem of rites remains. Ricci hoped that the historic Christian rites would eventually prevail. In a recent article a Chinese minister working in Taiwan (Formosa) asks whether Christian observances may not sometimes be enriched and made more relevant by borrowing from the traditional piety. He thinks

[8] For China, K. S. Latourette, *Expansion*, III, pp. 340-55, or more fully in his *History of Christian Missions in China* (SPCK, 1929), chaps. 6, 7, 8.

it unjust to forbid incense but to allow expensive flower wreaths (what would happen if a Chinese missionary told English mourners their flowers were signs of idolatry?), suggests that existing Christian burial rites fail to satisfy Chinese feelings, since they do not fulfil the criteria of propriety and filial piety expressed in the ancestor-ceremonies, and proposes a funeral service which would prove to the non-Christian that he is not being asked to stifle these good instincts. This is a simple illustration of a problem which is set far more acutely in other situations, for while he is confident that the worship of ancestors in any idolatrous sense is no longer implied in such ceremonies as the ancestor-tablets and the three bows, similar assumptions cannot be made in cultures nearer to their animistic inheritance. Presumably the answer is partly one of timing, to be decided by local knowledge, not rule-of-thumb. Thus it is significant that, according to this writer, Archbishop Yu Pin has told Taiwan Catholics that Ricci's line is now to be taken. Opposition to ancestor worship had been unfortunate. 'If anybody wants to prevent you from performing ceremonies to your ancestors, you come to me: I have the approval of Rome.'[*]

Next in the three capital sins came unchastity. Many moralists have been worried by Christian concentration upon sexual offences and by the harshness with which they have been treated. This is one factor in the modern revolt. Setting aside the plea that fornication is no sin at all, it is true that when only particular acts of sin are judged, it is impossible to say — as Christian discipline has so often implied — that an act of fornication is in itself more sinful than an act of cruelty or a theft. It may be impelled by love. But one element in the complex attitude of the Church towards the sexual instinct has been awareness, in line with all modern psychology, of its penetration into the depths of character and action. It is this which it tries to guide into right and fruitful expression, even when it uses disciplinary means and falls into

---

[*] Chow Lien-hwa, The Problem of Funeral Rites, in the *Occasional Bulletin* of the Overseas Council (Church Assembly 1963). For Shinto in Japan, R. Hammer, *Japan's Religious Ferment* (SCM Press, 1962).

legalistic traps. In addition, the society which early Christianity envisaged was rooted in the Christian family, and so the Church endeavoured by exhortation and discipline to guard marriage and the sanctities of the family. Whether or not this justifies in theory its concentration upon sexual offences, it goes far towards explaining its practice.

Though one cannot expect from the early Church a system of marriage law applicable to all circumstances, it is worth asking what can be learned from its experience in distinguishing moral and religious constants from practical and alterable rules of discipline.[10] Roman law distinguished *matrimonium justum*, which was strictly monogamous while it lasted but terminable by divorce, from other forms of union, more or less socially acceptable and subject to more or less legal disabilities. Nowadays divorce is a crucial moral and disciplinary issue, over which the laws of the Eastern and Western churches have differed from quite early times and Protestant churches differ again, causing perplexity in the younger churches. Here I take up only the matter of irregular unions.

The Church, unlike Roman law and social custom, objected to a married man having a concubine: this was adultery, punishable by excommunication. When an unmarried man had a concubine, it looked to the circumstances. First, Roman law prohibited full marriage, in some cases, between people of different social classes, and there was no marriage with or between slaves. It was therefore a bold step when Callistus recognized such unions as Christian marriage, provided the partners accepted its obligations. Secondly, the Church was compassionate towards the concubine who was faithful to the man who would or could not marry her, and who brought up her children with proper care. She was not disciplined for fornication. This has some analogy to the problem of polygamous wives. Third, the Church pressed successfully for improvement in the status of *concubinatus* in civil law. On the other hand it was anxious not to seem lax. Though a monogamous

[10] The literature is large and technical. I have found useful J. Gaudemet, *L'Eglise dans l'Empire Romain* (Paris, 1958), pp. 515-54.

concubinage was accepted as Christian marriage where there was a non-moral impediment to full legal marriage, it was disliked when the reason for not marrying was inadequate. For there was no guarantee of permanence; it was no true image of the marriage between Christ and his Church. The concubine might be dismissed, the family broken up. The guilty could then be disciplined; but, with no legal sanction to enforce it, the marriage might not be restored. So it was sometimes thought better at least to delay recognition: Augustine hesitates to baptize a concubine. The peril of over-tenderness is exposed by Caesarius when he says that concubinage before marriage is so common that custom does not count it sin and he, as bishop, cannot excommunicate for it, though he regards it as adultery. Fuller investigation of such points might assist consideration of modern problems like African customary marriage and polygamy, though no automatic solution is furnished by the early Church.

The attempt to prohibit mixed marriages deserves mention. In early times marriage with a pagan was thought to be grave sin (so Cyprian), even a form of adultery, deserving the same penalty (so Tertullian). As it became more common, councils forbade it, disciplining the parties or their parents, the father who gives his daughter to pagan, Jew or heretic. Augustine dissuades from it, but admits that it was not generally considered sinful and that the New Testament prescribes no rule. To Ambrose the husband is not lawfully coupled: the union will perhaps not be considered indissoluble, and can be no true fellowship. In changed circumstances later councils are more concerned about marriage with heretics. An African council forbids the sons and daughters of bishops and other clergy to marry heretics or schismatics; Chalcedon prohibits Readers from marrying heterodox women or Jews or pagans unless they promise to accept orthodoxy. Though this contrasts sharply with most modern Protestant practice, the constitutions of some younger churches contain clauses like this proposed for Nigeria: 'No minister of the Church may solemnize or bless the marriage of a Christian with a non-Christian.' Other points of interest are the early Church's attitude to betrothal (*sponsalia*), the significance of which it tried to deepen, and the equality of men and women in respect of chastity, quite contrary to Roman Law.

Polygamy has been a stumbling-block for centuries. St Basil used the word itself for successive marriages, which the Church then disliked: digamy, trigamy, polygamy; and the modern African may justly rebuke the older Christendom for the successive polygamy of its easy divorces. In the stricter sense, polygamy was already an issue for missionaries working among the Indians of Spanish America in the sixteenth century. There was a papal ruling that marriages before conversion, if legal by native custom, were to be held valid, and that a pagan with more than one wife must, before baptism, dismiss all but the one he first married – or, if he could not remember that, all but the one he liked best! More than a century ago Bishop Colenso of Natal was worried about such rules:

> The usual practice of enforcing the separation of wives from their husbands upon their conversion to Christianity is quite unwarrantable and opposed to the plain teaching of our Lord. It is putting new wine into old bottles and placing a stumbling-block, which he has not set, directly in the way of their receiving the Gospel.

Bishop Gray of Cape Town thought differently. In 1857 the African Samuel Crowther – soon to be Bishop on the Niger – argued from *Acts 15.28* 'for a general policy of demanding from converts seeking baptism no more than minimum qualifications necessary for salvation, leaving other refinements to time and their membership of the Church'; but Henry Venn was sure that God could not condemn polygamy in an old-established Church and tolerate it in a new one.[11]

The debate has continued:

> Insistence on a right to contract polygamous marriages is re-

---

[11] America: K. S. Latourette, *Expansion* III, p. 115; Colenso and Gray: G. W. Cox, *Life of Bishop Colenso* (1888) I, pp. 63-67; Crowther and Venn: J. F. A. Ajayi, *Christian Missions in Nigeria 1841-1891*, p. 106.

sponsible for most disciplinary expulsions from the churches, and for the setting-up of independent local sects.[12]

Though the historic churches cannot countenance new polyga-mous marriages after baptism, they vary in their rules concerning polygamous converts: some will not baptize them, some will baptize but not admit to communion, others admit to communion but not to office in the church. Already in 1857 the Baptist mis-sionary, T. J. Bowen, argued that commerce would create new standards of responsibility and remove one of the strongest props of polygamy, and many now believe that it is fast disappearing on economic grounds, helped by Christian teaching on the dignity of woman and the positive value of monogamy. Meanwhile the baffling disciplinary problem remains:

One congregation of a church which permits associate member-ship of those practising polygamy reports that not more than twenty to thirty couples out of a membership of a thousand can take Holy Communion.

With better understanding of the sociology of polygamy, which cannot be attributed merely to male lust (indeed there is a story of a Liberian chief who wanted to become a Christian because it was the only legal way to divorce twenty-two of his twenty-three wives), missionaries generally favour a milder discipline which would have seemed lax to most early Christians, yet is consistent with what we saw of many bishops' concern that disciplinary rules should not swamp pastoral care for the individual in his circum-stances.[13]

[12] T. Price, *African Marriage* (SCM Press, 1954), p. 22. This pamph-let discusses the implications of the *Survey of African Marriage and Family Life*, edited for the International Missionary Council by A. Phillips (OUP, 1953).

[13] Bowen: J. F. A. Ajayi, op. cit., p. 18. The quotation is from M. Marioghae and J. Ferguson, *Nigeria under the Cross* (CMS, 1965), p. 61, an example of a plea for sensitive discipline. Cf. E. Nida, *Cus-toms, Culture and Christianity* (Harper, 1954), p. 264: 'Polygamy is generally no longer treated by informed missionaries with shocked denunciation, but with an appreciative understanding of the numerous problems.' On its disappearance, B. A. Pauw, *Religion in a Tswana Chiefdom* (OUP, 1960), pp. 84, 93; E. Nida, op. cit., p. 105, with some statistics; J. V. Taylor, *Buganda*, p. 185.

IV

Some broad principles emerge for consideration.

1. Positive duties come first: to preach the Gospel of forgiveness and new creation in Christ, and to set forth the Christian way of life.

2. While this way must be fully Christian in principle, it cannot be imported *en bloc* as Law (or as Western culture), but has to be worked out to meet local cultures. As soon as possible the indigenous church should be responsibly engaged in interpreting Christianity in its own situation, making its own decisions under the guidance of the Holy Spirit.

3. Conversely, indigenous churches must recognize that they cannot interpret the Christian faith (even from the Bible) or their own cultures without the help of universal Christian thought and experience. This is not the same as being in bondage to the missionary.

4. Some discipline is inevitable. Its aim must be pastoral not punitive, and therefore directed towards the individual in his total personality and total circumstances. Tariffing offences is a crude method which may either 'protect the holiness of the Church' at the expense of souls if the penalties are severe, or cheapen true discipline if they are slight and mechanical. Legalism is always the enemy.[14] In particular, exclusion from Holy Communion should not be assumed to be the normal method of discipline. The catechumenate must be kept preparatory, not punitive.

5. The details of a disciplinary system need constant review, since they are relative to the changing environment and the stage of development of a local church. Discipline must not be a piece of clericalism, but should commend itself to the conscience of the whole congregation, even if this involves moving slowly and accepting some risks to the reputation of Christianity. Yet the clergy, as pastors, must often resist narrow and legalistic demands from the congregation, especially well-settled, respectable congre-

[14] For striking examples see M. B. Syrier, *Black Woman in Search of God* (Lutterworth Press, 1962), pp. 53-63: They always want a law.

gations. Understanding and compassion are pre-eminent in Christ himself. Truly salutary discipline is possible when the congregation supports the sinner, sharing in the sorrow of the penitent, praying for and with him, pointing forward to reconciliation. This is impossible if discipline is made trivial.

It is good to reflect on principles. It cannot be concealed, however, that the rub comes when they have to be applied. Discipline is exceedingly difficult. The Western churches of today are not in a good position to advise the younger churches, and are more likely to have something to learn from them. A uniform system would be quite wrong, even in a united Church. But increasing unity and common counsel will open us all to the Holy Spirit.

CHAPTER SIX

UNITY AND DIVISION

THERE ARE said to be over 250 denominations in the USA; that is modest compared with 2000 in South Africa. If elsewhere numbers are less high, they are striking enough: a year or two ago seventy-seven Independent churches were registered in Nigeria and 112 Christian groups in Japan. Why is this so, and what is to be done about it?

This theme is organic to the disciplinary matters already discussed in several ways. First, schisms or sects can spring from the same clash of cultures that engenders problems of discipline, from the convert's difficulty in understanding and assimilating a religion which has grown up in another culture and taken concrete form in a church whose institutions are in part shaped by that culture. Again, schisms can spring from concern for the holiness of the Church and the use of discipline to protect it. Or, to turn from origins to consequences, schisms give rise to disciplinary questions; fresh problems are set about the relations between denominations, and the solution of standing problems is hampered when the offender can run next door. While this is all true and important, I would not like to tie this discussion of unity and schism too closely to the issue of discipline in its technical sense, since disunity will not be overcome by disciplinary measures alone. Fragmentation of the one Church of Christ can only be conquered by attention to the whole situation, both to the causes which lead to schism (that is, by diagnosing the ill-health of the Church) and to the positive ideas of unity and wholeness (that is, by understanding the good health, the *salus*, of the Church).

I shall consider unity and schism in the early Church under four main heads: the causes of schism, the theology of unity and schism, the discipline of schism, the prevention and cure of schism. Then I come to the modern Church, taking examples mainly from Africa, and having the same four heads in mind, though I shall treat them less systematically.[1]

Part I: The Early Church

A. Causes of Schism

1. Personal

Unity may be disrupted when some individual, through ambition, pride or sense of grievance, defies authority, breaks communion or is expelled, finds sympathizers and forms a party; which becomes a schism, as the early Church understood it, when altar is set up against altar, bishop against bishop, when, in other words, the party organizes itself in the form of a church. In early days, when unity was taken seriously as a mark of the Church, a schism was not likely to gather much strength without a platform worth considering; and while leadership was important, it is hard to find instances of large and viable schismatic movements originating in purely personal dissensions. Five presbyters at Carthage, resenting the choice of Cyprian as bishop after his short experience as presbyter, formed a faction against him which subsequently took schismatic shape under a rival bishop. But by then they had adopted a view on the reconciliation of lapsed Christians which gave them, they thought, a *raison-d'être* as an opposition group. In Rome, at the same time, Novatian may not have advocated a rigorist discipline before he was disappointed of the bishopric, and many scholars think he then acted on personal grounds only. But I believe he was already disposed towards a stricter view than the new bishop's; and even if that is not so, there was plainly a

---

[1] Part I is based on my *Schism in the Early Church* (SCM Press, 2nd ed., 1964) in which fuller discussion and references to sources and modern literature can be found.

body of opinion which welcomed a lead in that direction. Personal ambition probably bulked large with Melitius who started a schism in Egypt that gave Athanasius much trouble, and some papal schisms look like personal quarrels. On the whole, however, it is a combination of personal motives with something else which we find. If that sounds obvious, it is less obviously true later on.

2. Dogmatic

Schism is often distinguished from heresy as a breach of unity which does not originate from, or turn much upon, unorthodoxy. Looked at another way, heresy becomes schismatic when the heretics form separated bodies claiming to be Christian churches. Christian theology *is* difficult. The teacher can put it out of proportion, the learner may grasp it inadequately. Some want it to be more philosophical, some less; some want it more sharply defined, some less. Some, as they teach or receive it, assimilate it to a preconceived world-view. Hence, in addition to settling particular controversies, certain over-all questions become urgent. By what standards is orthodoxy determined? Bible, Creed, conciliar definitions, tradition as expounded by authority? In the last case, by what authority? What risks can the Church take in safeguarding its faith? What room is there for liberty of opinion, what diversity of interpretation can be comprehended within the Church without compromising truth? Can we distinguish between doctrines and institutions necessary to salvation and those which, though objectively part of the truth and well-being of the Church, are not conditions of membership to which every individual must subscribe? If truth and charity clash, which has the higher claim? Is it better to hold on to the truth because fellowship without it is a sham, or to the fellowship because without it truth cannot be discovered or maintained? All this is so difficult that the large number of separated bodies whose existence rests upon a point of doctrine is not surprising. Their multitude is nothing new. In the fourth century Epiphanius listed about eighty and Filaster forced this up to 156. Though Augustine thought Filaster fanciful, he gives eighty-eight heretical groups in his own *De Haeresibus*.

3. Disproportionate emphasis on one or more elements in Christian life

A single example is better than enumeration, and I take Montanism. Montanus had been priest of the Mother Goddess in Phrygia. When he came forward as a Christian prophet (c. 170), he may have been driven by ambition or he may have wanted a more exciting and enthusiastic Christianity than he found, more like his former cult: we cannot say. But since his movement spread beyond Asia Minor into the West, it probably met some real need, and the suggestion that it reaffirmed, in however distorted a form, authentic elements in primitive Christianity is reasonable. On the evidence available, these included confidence in immediate guidance and enhanced power from the Holy Spirit to a degree and by means which had become abnormal (prophecy and visions were emphasized), expectation of the imminent return of Christ, and a pattern of life conditioned by this expectation, renouncing much that other Christians thought legitimate, especially marriage, and severely disciplined.

To call it a reaction against the growing institutionalism of the Church may be going too far. Yet the Church had been developing institutional authority against the Gnostic sects. With an almost settled Scripture and Rule of Faith, and with bishops whose doctrine and discipline must be accepted, there was danger that being a Christian would be equated with being a good churchman, a pious and obedient member of a saving institution. Tertullian rejoined by defining the Church in terms of 'spiritual men': the Church is the Spirit, not the bishops. Much in Montanism was wrong or absurd, and over against it there was need of a strong historic Church which could perpetuate that authentic apostolic Christianity which is itself the test of subjective experiences purporting to be immediate responses to the Spirit. That Montanism stood for something real, nevertheless, is suggested by the appearance throughout history of movements similar in principle, up to the Pentecostalists of today. They pose the question: How can the enthusiasm and loyalty which they engender be given proper expression within a sound institutional framework in which the proportion of Christian faith and life is preserved? And they ask, What is the cost of visible unity?

4. The holiness of the Church and the enforcement of discipline

This has been sufficiently illustrated in previous chapters. In Montanism rigorist discipline went with its eschatology. In Donatism it was one cause of schism among many. 'Whoever communicates with the traitors will have no part with us in the Kingdom of Heaven,' wrote the martyrs of Abitina from their prison. But personal quarrels, Numidian jealousy of Carthage, social unrest and regional or racial discontent with Rome, were also factors in this bitter struggle. Waiving its possible origin in ambition, Novatianism, once established, is a pure case of disciplinary schism. The true Church must be holy, its members must be holy in conduct. This communion of righteous saints is protected by discipline, serious relaxation of which corrupts the Church to the verge of destruction. Then the faithful and holy remnant breaks with the rest, preserves the discipline, and is alone the Catholic Church. This recurrent type of schism points an accusing finger at a slack Church and forces the problem, how to reconcile zeal for purity with compassion for the sinner within one healthy fellowship.

5. Problems of worship

Apart from controversies over the date and observance of Easter, the early Church managed to avoid serious divisions over worship. The accepted act of worship was the eucharist, and with minor exceptions the essential constituent elements of this sacrament were agreed. Given their use, variety in detail was permitted. In general, there was a desire to observe whatever had been instituted by the apostles, and sometimes difficulties cropped up as to what that might be. There were little dissident groups like the Aquarioli who refused to use wine in the eucharist. But broadly speaking, worship, unless complicated by theological

issues (in which case they are fundamental), does not appear as a
cause of schism with the same frequency and intensity as in later
times. It is noteworthy that there was no objection to the use of the
vernacular where desired. The common use of Greek or Latin,
however, may have helped unity.

6. Social, economic and political factors

These are difficult to distinguish and assess. That Eastern and
Western Churches began early to diverge from each other in
certain ways is clear. It must have been due partly to social and
cultural conditions and to politics, and is not necessarily bad, if
full fellowship is maintained. Evidence of Christianity's power to
become the religion and the civilizing force of very different
cultures and to find appropriate expression in them is welcome,
and whether it can exhibit this power universally is the great
question put to all missions.

More particularly, however, it is often asserted that the Donatist schism in Africa and the formation of separated churches in
the East during the Christological controversies are to be explained mainly by non-theological factors. Here caution is ad-
visable, for the reality of the theological or religious problems and
passions should not be underestimated; without them these divisions would not have happened. Still, it is clear that in the case of
Donatism, besides some personal quarrels, there was resentment
in Numidia of either the primacy of Carthage or the way it was
exercised; and, in the eastern controversies, that calm theological
discussion was frustrated by the rivalry and power politics of the
great sees, especially Alexandria and Constantinople, and by the
dislike of many Christians for a control from the capital (Constantinople) in which emperor and patriarch co-operated. So far,
this is trouble within the Church. Next, there was much social
discontent in Africa which could be canalized against landlords
felt to be somehow identified with a Roman upper-class supported
from Rome; and since the State, at Rome and in Africa, came out
against the Donatists, it may well be true that many poor Christians and many country folk (especially in Numidia), irked by

Roman control, favoured the Donatists for non-theological
reasons. It is not easy to distinguish between the religious and
political elements in the popular appeal of the Donatist claim to
be the church of the martyrs, since it was the State which perse-
cuted and the Catholics (their opponents argued) were now in with
the State. Whether to go one more step and call this nationalism is
a moot point. There is insufficient evidence, and some to the contrary, that the Donatist church as such or those who backed it on
social grounds wanted a separatist régime, political independence;
and even less likelihood that Christians in Egypt or Syria during
the fifth century wanted to see independent kingdoms established
there. So we must beware of reading political nationalism back
into the situation. Yet a strong regional consciousness, a diffused
feeling that they were too much under Constantinople's thumb,
could stimulate ecclesiastical loyalties and controversies even
where their roots were not political. This resembles what has certainly happened in later times.

B. Theology of Unity and Schism

The essential theology can be put briefly. Men sometimes
thought about an invisible Church, but not as an alternative to the
visible. The visible Church was one communion, and all other
bodies claiming to be Christian were outside the Church, whether
they were heretics or orthodox schismatics. The true Church
could be identified by its continuity with the apostles, and most
clearly by its apostolic Scriptures and apostolic Rule of Faith and
by the historically continuous local churches tracing their pedi-
gree back to apostolic founders or apostolic mother-churches. Of
this historic continuity the continuous ministry in each church
was both evidence and organ. Proof was found in the known
successions of bishops holding office in each see from apostolic
times: all the bishops of Rome, Ephesus, Antioch. It was the
bishop's duty to maintain continuity of faith and practice; God
helped him to do this. Outside these apostolic successions there
was no guarantee of authentic Christianity.

Constructed against Gnosticism, this argument lay ready at hand against the rigorist schismatics, and was strengthened by fuller exposition of the objective character of the Church's holiness, namely the Spirit's presence in this body and the apostolic Church's mediation of holiness through objective sacraments. This all crystallized into the theology associated with Cyprian: *Extra ecclesiam nulla salus.* Outside this identifiable, visible, single, historic Church there is no action of the Holy Spirit, no ministry, no baptism, no eucharist, no salvation. Accordingly, schismatic bodies also, like the Novatianists and Donatists, claimed to be not one church among others, but the only Church. There was debate about the means of recognizing the Church and about qualifying the strictest teaching on what happens outside the Church. But with scanty exception there was no belief that the one Church might comprise several churches or denominations, out of communion with one another yet all being church and possessing ministries and sacraments through which the Holy Spirit worked unto salvation. Further tests of the one true Church were seen in its universality over against the particularism of the sects. This was argued geographically — how could the Donatists in a corner of Africa be the catholic Church, prophesied and promised as the Church of all nations? And dogmatically — how could the opinions of a splinter group hold against the agreement of the apostolic churches everywhere? Though these arguments are not watertight, they carry weight and were tenaciously propounded. They were the theological norm.

It was hard to maintain this doctrine in its most uncompromising form, since heretics and schismatics are not pagans. Consequently, against Cyprian's teaching, it came to be allowed that where sacraments had been administered with the correct matter and form (to use later terms), they were in some sense valid; something had happened which could not be undone and need not be repeated. So baptism and ordination outside the Church were counted valid. But these were not thought to make a church: they were inefficacious until the recipient entered the true Church in which alone the Holy Spirit works. Theologically these concessions are an unsatisfactory compromise from which one must retreat or advance, but in preventing and in healing schism this theological position has great power. Unity is divine, necessary and precious. Break it at your peril. How can schismatic action be the fruit of love? And if you have not love, you have nothing profitable, certainly not the Holy Spirit. It is a tricky argument, but telling. One must admire the early Church's sense of the theological imperative of unity.

C. The Discipline of Schism

You cannot discipline someone who has left your communion unless he wants to return. Still, there were points of discipline occasioned by schism. Marriage with schismatics was sometimes forbidden or disciplined, conditions of return were laid down, and the ecclesiastical consequences of the theological recognition of valid sacraments outside the Church had to be worked out. These were important. What baptisms should be accepted? The Western answer was simple: all those in which the right form and matter are used, that is, water and the invocation of the Trinity, since the Lord will then have acted upon his promises. The East made more distinctions among schismatic bodies, holding rather that the Church may decide what to legitimize after consideration of each case, though correct form and matter will count heavily. This difference in outlook is significant for later discussions, since the Western view turns on the intrinsic nature of the sacrament, the eastern more upon the body which dispenses it. The other big question was, What is still required for one baptized in schism who wants to join the Catholic Church? The answer, reception with the laying-on of the bishop's hand, whereupon the baptism becomes effective through the Holy Spirit within the Church. It seems incorrect to regard this as confirmation: it is rather the reconciliation of a penitent. But in time it perhaps came to be thought of as confirmation.

Acceptance of those ordained in schism as clergy within the Church raised a prior question. Strictly, it had been held, none who passed through public discipline could be ordained or, if already ordained, continue to minister. However, it was found possible to dispense from that rule or to by-pass it by not submitting such men formally to penance. Then, for those who accepted the argument developed by Augustine, they could be received as ministers already ordained. In the East, and for a time in parts of the West, it was less simple. They were received with an imposition of hands which is difficult to interpret, like the 'more mystical ordination' administered to Melitian clergy and the ambiguous imposition of hands upon Novatianists, both by decision of Nicaea. Certainly some theologians regarded these as ordination (or reordination, if we must use the word). Others may have availed themselves of a deliberate ambiguity, trusting that the future status of the ministers within the Church was assured. If so, the modern parallel in the reunion plans of the Ceylon, N. Indian, Anglican–Methodist, Nigerian or Canadian type is striking.

It remains to say that there was no positive discipline concerning relations between churches, no intercommunion regulations, since plurality of churches was not recognized, though there was an interesting, if intermittent, tenderness for the Novatianists.

D. Prevention and Cure of Schism

Here the chief measure in the early Church was its unremitting insistence upon a positive concept of unity (in the theology described above), accompanied by pastoral exhortation to keep the fellowship — almost above all else. When schism occurred, the theological concessions already mentioned helped: men need not admit they had never been baptized, ministers could continue their ministry without repudiating their ordination. Further, although relations between catholics and heretics or schismatics were often harsh to the point of bloodshed, there were sometimes attempts at 'dialogue'. Athanasius's Council of Alexandria (362), when Nicenes and 'Semi-Arians' came to a better understanding, and Augustine's conferences with Donatists are good instances of what may have been commoner than we know. And there were the efforts, not always conciliatory, of the major Councils. On the other hand, the Church never did heal some of the greatest breaches of unity, particularly the terrible divisions in the East associated with Christological controversy, while some of those which were more or less absorbed came to their end through sheer weariness or change in outward circumstances — like barbarian invasions — or by coercion, when the Church requested or consented to legislation and secular sanctions to suppress schism. That the State had a duty to keep order and that some schisms, notably Donatism, fostered social discontent and used violence must be admitted. But that the same Church which under persecution had forcefully stated the principles of religious liberty should have turned to coercion and tried to justify it in theory was a moral and theological tragedy with untold consequences for evil. Certainly not the right way to deal with schism.

Part II: Modern Churches

With a reminder that the great East–West schism happened long before the Reformation, I come to the Church of today and our unhappy divisions. In addition to the old causes of schism we are faced with long-standing divisions inherited by people who think little, if at all, about their causes, divisions now spread over the world by missions sometimes in competition, and cross-fertilized so as to produce new sects. Nor is this only a fact; it is allied with a principle, or two principles, one good, one bad. Respect for individual conscience, for honest convictions, for the responsibility which needs freedom, is good. Contented acceptance of disunity, failure to see it as a scandal to the world and an injury to the one Christ, is bad. While Protestants can fairly say that the possible forms of unity require investigation, and may feel that the argument from Catholic unity is sometimes pressed against them unfairly or that episcopacy in apostolic succession is no guarantee against schism, it is impossible to shut one's eyes to the fissiparousness of Protestantism, the dissidence of dissent. When there are twenty denominations in a city, why not twenty-one, or 121? Thus splits are not checked by a dominating principle that honest differences must if possible be comprehended within unity.

We may now review the causes of schism in their modern setting.

1. Personal

The personal factor has come more to the front, though this is not proved merely by the occurrence of names like Lutheranism, Calvinism, Wesleyanism, which stand for complex theological positions and religious insights; and one does not know what private ambition lies behind some denominations whose titles lay claim to catholicity. A classic case-study is Bengt Sundkler's *Bantu Prophets in South Africa*, in which he shows how many splits issue from no other apparent cause than someone's desire to be a leader and exercise power. This he traces to the suppression of African ability for leadership in other spheres of South African society. To this there was little parallel in the early Church which often worked the other way, taking as leaders men who had proved themselves in secular society. In nineteenth-century England the Free Churches often developed men's capacity for leadership which passed on into social and political movements. So, although ambition is to be found everywhere, the frequency of leadership-schism is related to the social structure of a region or State. Pauw says of the Tswana chiefdom which he studied: 'The opportunities for leadership in the churches now make up for the loss of such opportunities in the political and administrative sphere.' Wishlade, writing recently of southern Malawi, says the same, though there he has not found the colour bar in itself to be a cause of sectarianism. Desire to be a leader and acquire a following is only one factor in the multiplication of sects, but in places a considerable one. Better secular opportunities might reduce the temptation. There is also the desire of a small community to be free from any centralized ecclesiastical control, from

any formal obligation beyond themselves, and the simple longing
for something quite their own, perhaps a church building run by
themselves in their own way, with the warmth, loyalty and pride
thereby nourished. This feeling should find satisfaction within the
larger community, but frequently it does not.[2]

2. Doctrinal

If there is now less controversy over some dogmas than in the
early Church, there is more over others. Most obvious are the new
problems set by science, philosophy and psychology and by biblical criticism. While some churches have managed to contain
within themselves fundamentalist and critical approaches to
Scripture, there are many separate churches whose principal
raison d'être is biblical fundamentalism or some particular tenet
derived from an uncritical biblicism. Case-studies of Africa amply
illustrate this. Dr Taylor hammers it home in his study of Buganda.
We have reached the point where, just as Rome is striving to become more scriptural, Protestants are compelled to reconsider the
meaning and authority of tradition.[3] Lack of balance in presenting
the faith, disproportionate or exclusive attention to single themes,
spring readily from uncontrolled use of the Bible. Many sects stake
everything on baptism (some making total immersion essential),
some concentrate on healing, some are sabbatarian, and so forth.
Syncretism also, though no new problem, is one of renewed
gravity, whether a church faces a great historic religion or an
animistic society. The case-studies reveal how often sects appear
by secession from a mother-church which cannot go as far as some
wish in assimilating ancient beliefs and practices. Some sects may,
to put it rather unchristianly, be useful experiments in assimila-

[2] B. G. M. Sundkler, Bantu Prophets in South Africa (Lutterworth
Press, 1948; 2nd ed., Oxford University Press, 1961); B. A. Pauw,
Religion in a Tswana Chiefdom (OUP, 1960); R. L. Wishlade, Sectarianism in Southern Nyasaland (OUP, 1965). See also F. B. Welbourn, East African Rebels (SCM Press, 1961) and V. E. W. Hayward,
ed., African Independent Church Movements (Edinburgh House Press,
1963), the last with extensive bibliography.
[3] J. V. Taylor, Buganda, pp. 219-20, 238-43; cf. B. G. M. Sundkler,
Bantu Prophets, pp. 275-78.

tion, while others become bridges back towards something only marginally Christian, much as happened with Gnosticism in early days.

3. Holiness and Discipline

Holiness or perfectionist denominations have been common in America and have thence been propagated by active missionaries; and many have sprung up more or less spontaneously. Some of them seek perfection in a general way; others, as in the early Church, make one or more points of discipline their indispensable touchstone of holiness and impose a way of life which is legalistic, or may easily become so, as well as perfectionist, and is often associated with biblical fundamentalism. Thus in Asia as in Africa older tabus are replaced by the prohibition of alcohol or tobacco or pork — these tabus imported from America. The discipline may be useful, yet the underlying theology harmful. Such bodies tend to be exclusive, though exclusiveness may be offset by the leader's desire for a larger following. Since the older mission churches, Catholic or Protestant, can more easily risk losses by imposing penalties, they may in practice be the more exclusive and legalistic. The Ethiopian Church in Malawi, says Wishlade, is known to outsiders as the 'Do Bad Things Church', the church which ignores the rules of the missionaries; among other things it permits polygamy.

Revivalist elements often go with perfectionist, with their emphasis upon the immediate impact of the Holy Spirit. Pentecostalist movements have to be taken seriously in any assessment of the total Christian situation. They are powerful in America North and South, active in Asia and Africa as missionaries, and give rise by their example to many similar, but independent, sects. The parallel with Montanism is often striking, especially in Africa. They are strongly eschatological or millenarian, they are ruled by prophets, they accept revelation through dreams and ecstasy. They need not be unorthodox, but distortion and superstition are likely, and they are buttressed by a distinctive discipline. A special feature — not the mark of any one body in the early Church, but certainly an element in early Christianity—is emphasis upon divine healing through prayer, exorcism and purificatory rites. From this general group, commonly called Zionist in Africa from its original association with Zion City, Illinois, Sundkler and others now distinguish the Messianic sects in which the leader or prophet is regarded as Messiah, and he, rather than the 'Jesus of the Book', is the way to God or God's way to man—the Gate. There is a hazy border-territory between a kind of identification with the real Christ which might not be unorthodox and a substitution of the Messiah for Christ which is outside historic Christianity—again a parallel with Montanus and the Paraclete. The problem is to satisfy what emotions and other needs should be satisfied, and to use leadership, enthusiasm, faith and hope within the historic Church without travestying authentic Christianity.[4]

4. Worship

There is no *a priori* reason why Western forms should satisfy other peoples. They may, if people are conditioned to them; but in many places they do not. How many sects have come into being in order to worship differently I cannot say, but this is a motive readily linked up with others. It must be sufficient here to distinguish between indigenization, which is normally to be desired and frequently demands a richer, more dramatic worship than Western Protestants favour, and syncretization, where unchristian ideas are expressed in the worship. Other points to be noted from African studies are (i) stress on healing in the context of worship, almost monopolizing it, (ii) comparative neglect of the eucharist, despite love of ceremonial and drama and the tradition of sacred feasts. Occasionally it is repudiated as an invention of the white man, or even the Devil.

5. Social, economic and political factors

The relation between social structure and modern denominationalism is frequently studied, and since sociology is popular,

[4] Cf. footnote (2) and D. Webster, *Pentecostalism and Speaking with Tongues* (Highway Press, 1965).

theological reasons for secessions and sects may now be under-estimated. But few doubt the importance of non-theological factors. People like to get together with others of their kind for the activities which cluster round church or chapel. Economic reasons reinforce social: there was a time when the poor in great English cities did not feel at home in church because they wore the wrong clothes or could not pay for a pew. Chapel offered an alternative. Plurality of denominations is then defended theologic-ally by pleas that the unity of the Church is spiritual and does not require uniformity.

When racial distinctions and political pressures are added, you get the 2000 Bantu sects, with one large group of sects (commonly called Ethiopian) actuated primarily by the desire for independ-ence of all that is white or Western. In their orthodoxy, education, attitude to African traditions and degree of syncretism, they differ greatly one from another, as well as in the kind of independ-ence they seek. Some accept *apartheid* because it enhances their separation and independence as churches. But, as Sundkler's second edition shows, they may overcome some of their internal dissensions. They are an extreme case, due to exceptional circum-stances, of what was seen in Donatism and in the Separated Eastern Churches.[5]

The prevention and cure of fragmentation may now be allowed to cover the theological and disciplinary matters which I took separately when speaking of the early Church. First, we repudiate coercion. The State has a duty to maintain public order and may have to take action against movements proved to be subversive or seditious; sometimes Christians will suffer through misjudgment. It may also have rights concerning land and buildings, and may require registration of groups and corporations, as often in Africa, or trust-deeds, as is normal everywhere. Plainly the historic churches should not take advantage of this to manoeuvre against sects; here the early Church after Constantine set no good ex-

[5] Ethiopian churches, V. E. W. Hayward, op. cit., *passim* and biblio-graphy; possible change discussed in B. G. M. Sundkler, op. cit., pp. 298-306, 314.

ample. More subtle is the temptation to coerce because it works. The Japanese government tried to force the denominations into a single church. In Australasia comity of missions has at times been enforced not by agreement, but by the strong hand of the government. In 1959 the South African Government ordered that church sites occupied by unrecognized churches in urban localities should be vacated. This drove some separatist bodies to join up either with a Mission church or with one another, and extinguished others. Whether or not the State's action was justified, this is not the Church's way to unity. One remembers how Augustine, who once championed toleration, was converted to 'Compel them to come in' by what he deemed good evidence that anti-Donatist legislation had worked — one of the saddest conversions of history.[6]

Let us then turn to church action. In this context discipline of the individual is marginal, and proselytizing will not achieve large-scale unity. We are dealing with groups, with denominations.

First, grievances and frustrations must be understood and where possible removed. Economic, social and racial grievances can hardly be removed except by the State or society at large. The historic churches must at least be known to act in the right direction. There are also specifically ecclesiastical dissatisfactions to be met and gaps to be filled. Behind many sects is the need for indigenization and responsible self-government, and for the satisfaction of genuine talent for leadership, lay or clerical. Next, what is good in the impulse behind holiness and pentecostal sects has to find place in the churches as part of a richer whole. The Revival movement in East Africa, though open to some criticism, shows that something along these lines can be profitably contained within the Church. The same will be true of traditional or national cultures: not that the problems can be solved by fitting little bits of tradition into an existing Western pattern, but that it must somehow be possible for Christianity to find expression in various

[6] South African government policy, B. G. M. Sundkler, op. cit., pp. 65-79 and the chapter added to the second edition.

cultures, since this has happened fairly successfully in the past.[7]

Secondly, this is all so difficult that it requires unflagging top-level study (which it is now getting) and a vigorous educational programme. No doubt all our Christianity is imperfect. Yet it is not supercilious to say that the Christianity of many sects is grievously distorted. In particular, as is widely acknowledged, the Bible is grossly misused; there must be sober Bible teaching, suitable commentaries and guides to study. Simultaneously, there must be propagated some sense of the place of order, continuity, tradition, in Christian life, a sense of the relevance of the history of the whole Church to each part. That should also help to clarify the distinction between Christianity as such and Western culture.

But how? It sounds Utopian, since the sectarians are not under the control of the historic churches. But according to Sundkler and others there are signs that leaders of many independent churches are open to such assistance, provided they are treated as friends. The modern dialogue between the greater churches must be extended. Further, the older churches must provide examples of (i) successful unifications across stiff barriers, and (ii) genuine unity without uniformity; always easier to say than do. Only positive demonstration of the power of Christian unity and of the interdependence of unity and mission can sufficiently counteract the heady delights of sectarianism. Next, the practical examples of friendship and unity both need a theological foundation. For first, since to offer friendship to sectarians must lead to invitations to co-operation and membership in various councils, this will force the theological question of the marks and boundaries of the Church, of intercommunion before corporate unity, of recognition of diverse ministries and baptisms. This is the theology of disunity. We saw how tentatively the early Church stepped from the severe position of Cyprian towards a theology of valid, but not effica-cious, ministries and sacraments outside the Church. Subsequently the idea has been turned topsy-turvy, for now they are often counted efficacious but not valid, according to circumstances.

[7] On the Revival movement, M. A. C. Warren, *Revival* (SCM Press, 1954); F. B. Welbourn, *East African Christian* (OUP, 1965, pp. 141-51).

Without pressing my own conclusions, I would stress the necessity of a working theology of disunity. We are seeing Rome itself turning towards one.

But secondly, a theology of disunity, necessarily anomalous, can only be evolved from a theology of unity, of what the Church truly is in Christ and should make visible. It must be shown how the Church is held together in Christ by objective bonds: Bible, creed, sacraments and (as most think) ordained ministry. It means relating these binding elements to the freedom of Christ and the Spirit who address us now. It means balancing authority with freedom and estimating the practicable and honest limits of comprehension. Problems everywhere. My point is the necessity of ecumenical theology.[8] Hard as this is, new hope is offered to us. Complacency is being broken down, so many people and churches are looking beyond self-defence towards mutual enrichment and wholeness. Moreover, wholeness is not being sought only in the past. We look forward to a wholeness or catholicity grounded in the historical revelation in Christ, but actualized by the living Christ through the growing experience of more kinds of Christian as Mission and Unity come properly together. We are not trying to preserve either primitive Graeco-Roman Christianity or primitive African culture, nor the sixteenth or nineteenth century forms of the Church. Older and younger churches? The whole Church is still having its growing-pains.

[8] For a general account, N. Goodall, *The Ecumenical Movement* (OUP, 1960).

INDEX